#Travelling With CARDBOARD PAUL

Keeping Promises whilst Travelling around the World

MICHELLE BOURKE

First published by Busybird Publishing 2019
Copyright © 2019 Michelle Bourke

ISBN
Print: 978-1-925949-02-5
Ebook: 978-1-925949-03-2

Michelle Bourke has asserted her right under the Copyright, Designs and Patents Act 1988 to be identified as the author of this work. The information in this book is based on the author's experiences and opinions. The publisher specifically disclaims responsibility for any adverse consequences, which may result from use of the information contained herein. Permission to use information has been sought by the author. Any breaches will be rectified in further editions of the book.

All rights reserved. No part of this publication may be reproduced, stored in or introduced into a retrieval system, or transmitted in any form, or by any means (electronic, mechanical, photocopying, recording or otherwise) without the prior written permission of the author. Any person who does any unauthorised act in relation to this publication may be liable to criminal prosecution and civil claims for damages. Enquiries should be made through the publisher.

Cover image: Kev Howlett, Busybird Publishing
Cover design: Busybird Publishing
Layout and typesetting: Busybird Publishing
Editor: Josephine Hong

Busybird Publishing
2/118 Para Road
Montmorency, Victoria
Australia 3094
www.busybird.com.au

Dedication

To my family and friends that came along for the ride and supported me on my escapades.

To Alyssa, thank you for organising and booking this *#tripofalifetime*.

To all the gorgeous people that I met along the way – especially those on the tours – that accepted Cardboard Paul as a fellow traveller. A special thank you to Pauline my sister from another mother who I met on the USA tour and became my life long tour buddy, friend, photographer and publicist.

To Paul, my gorgeous soul mate, who started me on this journey and gave me the idea of travelling with him and keeping promises.

My Darling Paul, even in death you continue to make me smile and laugh – even if you are a cardboard cut-out.

Always remembered,

Always loved.

Contents

Introduction	i
1. Our Journey Begins	1
2. Los Angeles	15
3. Las Vegas	29
4. San Francisco	45
5. New York	61
6. Texas	79
7. Paris	95
8. London	107
9. Great Britain	119
10. Ireland	141
11. Singapore	173
12. Homeward Bound and Beyond	183
About the Author	189

Introduction

Whilst travelling on the *#tripofalifetime*, I was fortunate to keep a promise I had made.

In early 2016 after my husband, Paul, received a terminal diagnosis with months left to live, we started planning.

The realisation that the love of my life would be gone was devastating – especially since he was still relatively young and we were in the midst of our plans to travel the world and grow old together.

When Paul became seriously ill towards the end of his life, he asked me what I would do when he was gone. I told him that I would travel to all the places that we had planned on visiting. I explained that I would get a life-size cardboard cut-out of him, pack him in my suitcase, take him travelling with me, and take photos of us at all the tourist destinations. He didn't believe me, but I promised him I would.

Fortunately, I had the opportunity to keep that promise to Paul when I booked a nine weeks tour around the USA and Europe from August to October 2017. I originally booked tickets to see Paul McCartney in concert in the USA, one in New Jersey and the other at Madison Square Garden, New York City and it snowballed from there.

A few months prior to leaving for my trip, I made preparations to have a cardboard cut-out of Paul to take along with me. I found a supplier that custom-made cardboard cut-outs and within 48 hours of placing my order, Cardboard Paul arrived. He was made from a photo taken on our wedding day – the only suitable photo I could find of Paul standing by himself. Cardboard Paul stood at 5 feet 9 inches, a young-looking 36 year-old spunk. When I put Cardboard Paul up, our dog, Ollie, started barking at him. I took some photos and put them up on Facebook. After Paul's passing, I was interviewed on *AM Healing My Soul TV* to talk about grieving and reinventing my life after Paul's death. We later had a special update on the arrival of Cardboard Paul.

While preparing for my trip, I was concerned about fitting Cardboard Paul into my suitcase and had to find a bag big enough to fit him. After searching through my wardrobe, I found a large calico bag which fitted Cardboard Paul perfectly and into my suitcase effortlessly with no issues.

When people from the outside talk about grief, they make assumptions about what is going on in your life. What bothers me is not what they say but how they judge or label you. No one knows how I feel or what I am going through, only me. I found this quote that really resonates with me:

Before you assume, learn the facts

Before you judge, understand why

Before you hurt someone, feel

Before you speak, think.

I grieved with Paul when he was alive, we grieved for all the moments lost, all the travel we would have done together, all the laughter, conversations and togetherness we would no longer be able to share. I miss Paul and our conversations every day but that does not stop me from living my life. I have had to reinvent my life without Paul. Just because I travelled around the world with a cardboard cut-out of Paul doesn't mean I am grieving Paul and can't let him go.

In my late teens, I knew that there was something bigger than me. I became aware of my spirituality but didn't know what that meant. I knew there was something greater but I wasn't quite sure what was there. Strange things were happening to me that I couldn't explain.

Introduction

Apparitions and ghosts started appearing at the end of my bed. Occasionally, the bed would shake and I would wake up thinking there was an earthquake during the night.

From these experiences, I had an inner knowing and gut feeling that I would always follow. If it didn't feel right in my gut, I wouldn't put myself in the situation. For over 30 years I have followed that inner knowing and went on to develop my spiritual gifts and became a trans-medium connecting with my own team of spiritual guides that provide guidance with backing and support. Although I have accepted that Paul is no longer here in my life and in the physical world, I know that he is with me in spirit as I still have conversations with him and feel him around me occasionally.

The idea of travelling with a cardboard cut-out of Paul was based on a promise I made to him, a promise is a promise – plus we both had a wicked sense of humour. Paul was extremely witty and funny, he always tried to make people laugh. At the dinner table each night, it became a standing joke of who could make the other person laugh. Paul would normally win that one, especially when the kids were younger. Paul would always try and think of a funny line or situation when a particular topic was discussed, the more you laughed the more you fuelled his witty lines or dad jokes.

When I told Paul I was going to take a cardboard version of him travelling with me, he gave a big smile filled with both humour and disbelief – I had outwitted him but he couldn't believe I had the guts to go ahead with it.

On my journey around the world, I know that Paul was with me and thought my high jinks of travelling with him as a cardboard cut-out was spectacular – especially if he saw people's reactions, he would be chuckling to himself.

A major purpose of travelling with Cardboard Paul was to show people that life still goes on and doesn't stop when our loved ones leave us. What a wonderful gesture to honour someone you love. On my travels, not only was I creating memories for myself, but also for those that crossed our path. Hopefully, those are memories that they will cherish and smile back upon.

Plus, it was so much fun.

Life continues whether we are in it or not. It's too short and amazing to stop living. I take every opportunity to live life to the fullest and enjoy every single moment.

Still being able to communicate with Paul from the other side, he sent a message recently stating, 'If I had only known then what I know now, I would have lived differently.'

I am certainly continuing to live differently since Paul has passed. After visiting seven countries and travelling on the *#tripofalifetime* with the *#mosttravelledcardboardcutout*, I wrote this story about my journey *#travellingwithcardboardpaul* – keeping promises whilst moving forward.

Here is my story.

1
Our Journey Begins

Melbourne to Los Angeles

My first time travelling overseas on my own was rather daunting as I was not quite sure what was going to happen, so I just went with the flow.

It was a huge relief when I was able to pack Cardboard Paul nicely and snugly into my suitcase. I received constant remarks of, 'Does he need a passport?' 'Have you booked him a seat?' 'He won't eat much', and 'He is very quiet'. My other concern was if I was called out at customs, what would I say when I had to unpack my suitcase and uncover Cardboard Paul. To my relief, it was hassle-free, though it would have been very interesting to see the face of those checking the security screens when my case went through the X-ray scanner.

A few days prior to travelling, I visited a friend that works with Australia Bush Flower Essences and she put a blend together to help with travelling and anxiousness on the plane – it helped to calm my nervous system and relieve jet lag.

I was flying out on Thursday, 24 August 2017 and started packing my suitcase the day before. I had a fair idea of what I was taking, so I was able to pack my bag quickly. Ollie, our dog, was lying on my bed watching me. He knew what was going on and felt sad that I was leaving him, although he didn't know for how long. I wasn't sure which of us was going to miss the other more.

My flight was departing around 9.30 am, so I had to be at the airport at least two hours beforehand. Matthew, my son, dropped me off at Tullamarine airport at 7.00 am, we hugged and said our goodbyes on the sidewalk and waved goodbye again as he drove off.

As I headed for the airport, I felt great anticipation but also anxious and slightly ill – luckily, I didn't eat breakfast beforehand. This is a common feeling I have when travelling.

I dragged my suitcase and carry-on luggage with me to the United Airlines check-in counter. There was a long queue and whilst I was waiting, I started chatting with a lady beside me and we discussed where we were travelling to. It seemed that we were going on the same tour and that she was travelling with a friend. I had met my first friend on this travel journey, Milva, and later on, Maria.

It took about twenty minutes to get through the queue and once I arrived at the end there was an attendant asking the same questions, 'Where are you travelling to? Have you a visa?'

When I finally got to the counter and placed my bag on the scales, I was very pleased to know that my luggage weighed around 18 kg, considering I had a limit of 23 kg. The attendant also commented that my luggage would be easy to spot. I had previously purchased a cover for my suitcase that had the words 'Paris' printed on it with pictures of the Eiffel Tower and other Parisian monuments. Yes, it would be very easy to spot on the luggage carousel.

Once I off-loaded my luggage, I walked to the international departure gate and whilst dodging people in the area that were taking selfies and group photos, I was able to get a selfie of myself. Once I had my photo opportunity, it was time to walk through the departure doors. Considering it was my first time travelling overseas in twenty-six years, I wasn't sure what to expect.

I showed my boarding pass and passport to the security officer guarding the departure doors, and once through I was confronted with large crowds of people and long queues to go through security check. A black Labrador sniffer dog was being led through the line of people and he stopped right next to me. I immediately said, 'Nope, I don't have any drugs on me.'

The security officer then asked how much cash I had on my person.

I said, 'Three hundred US dollars' – which was in my money belt.

He said, 'Fine, all good,' and praised the dog. *Phew*, I was starting to sweat over that one.

1. Our Journey Begins

When I finally got to the front of the queue, the security officer was asking more questions. 'Where are you going? What are you doing? How long are you away for?'

I unpacked my laptop from its case and put them and the rest of my carry-on luggage on the conveyor belt to go through the X-ray machine. Stuff was going everywhere, which didn't help my anxiety.

Whilst my luggage was going through the scanner, I, too, had to go through this very sophisticated upmarket machinery that scanned your whole body. You walk barefoot into a clear capsule and stand in position with your hands up and legs apart. It was very scary and daunting all at the same time. It makes you feel like a criminal – but this was not the only time I was made to feel like a criminal.

Once I went through the scanner, I collected my belongings and put my shoes back on.

Travelling with a laptop was not easy as it had to be unpacked and then repacked at the security check. This was a very good lesson I learnt about travelling: only packing and taking items that are useful.

I took a small laptop to write this book whilst travelling with Cardboard Paul, but eventually only sat down in New York and Paris to make notes, and on the boat to Ireland to upload photos. Instead of a laptop, next time I would look at smaller options like an iPad and a notebook.

Fortunately, I didn't have any issues going through customs – no alarms going off or being pulled aside for further interrogation.

Finally through customs, I headed towards my departure gate. I realised that I needed every bit of that two and half hours of arriving early to the airport. By the time I arrived at the gate, there wasn't much time left and I still hadn't eaten. I had a few snacks in my bag and purchased some water but that was it. I was certainly hoping that food was served earlier than later on the plane.

This was it, I thought to myself. Queuing to get on the plane that was going to take me to Los Angeles. Although I was not really looking forward to spending eleven hours on the plane, I was getting excited.

I was fortunate enough to have an aisle seat which is very important if you are in cattle class/economy on a long-haul flight. Melbourne to Los Angeles was eleven hours, so I was able to get up, walk around and go to the toilet without disturbing anyone. I was drinking lots of water, so I needed to use the bathroom often.

I sat beside two lovely, young Australian girls who were transiting in Los Angeles and then flying to Houston, Texas. One of them started chatting with me and told me that she met a young man who was living in New Orleans. She was living with him but had to fly back every eight weeks due to her visitor's visa. They had set up house together and she was hoping to get a more permanent visa as she was working two jobs and helping pay the rent.

We were a couple of hours into the flight and it became pitch black outside, which was a surprise as I knew it was the middle of the afternoon.

To pass the time, I ate, drank and watched *HGTV* – an American channel on house renovations and relocations. I was only able to sleep for a few hours, I felt uncomfortable sleeping upright and was trying not to snore and dribble.

I finally arrived at Los Angeles International Airport and waited patiently whilst other passengers grabbed their belongings and shuffled out of the airplane. The two ladies beside me bolted out of the plane as they were rushing to catch their connecting flight.

Walking through an airport you have never been before can be unnerving as I wasn't sure where I was going. I sheepishly followed the rest of the passengers hoping they knew where they were going.

As usual, once I got off the plane, I headed straight for the nearest toilets – it is usually a while since the last bathroom visit when getting

1. Our Journey Begins

off long flights. That was a very interesting experience as all the toilets were different to what I was used to – the toilet bowl was half full of water and when you flush, the bowl first fills up with water, then flushes down the pipe. All of the toilets had automatic flush sensors and if you moved, the toilet would flush, which wasn't pleasant if you were still sitting on it.

I got off the plane feeling exhausted, hungry, excited and anxious, all at the same time. When I found my way out and made my way to the USA customs, the experience was very interesting to say the least. In fact, it felt horrible. No one smiled and I didn't feel welcomed into the country at all.

There were many checks coming into the USA. Going through the first passport check, they asked the usual questions, 'Is your visit personal or business? How long will you be in the USA?' Your passport is stamped and they take your photo and scan your thumbprint for their records.

From the customs check, I then went to the baggage claim to collect my luggage which was easy to find as I was the only one with the bright Paris print luggage.

Once past the first section with luggage in hand, I was lining up to go through the next stage of customs. Whilst waiting in the queue, I spoke to a lady standing beside me and commented on my experience going through the first stage of customs. I commented on how rude they were and she agreed with me.

It wasn't the best welcome to the country where tourism is very important. It seemed as though they treated those coming into their country like criminals. I understand that they have to do their jobs, but there is no excuse for rudeness.

This time, they asked similar questions as the first customs check, checked my passport and thumbprint and let me through – I was finally free to explore the country.

Day 1 – Los Angeles

*A*s part of the tour, transportation to the hotel was organised. Before leaving the airport, I managed to catch up with Milva and Maria who were staying at another hotel just for a night before coming over to stay at the tour-designated hotel. I was on my way to the arranged hotel. Yes, I flew on a Thursday in Australia, and I went back in time and gained another Thursday in the USA.

When I finally arrived in LA, it was huge and smoggy. I felt confused which can be understandable after my long flight and lack of sleep.

I was dropped off at a hotel in downtown LA and proceeded to the reception to see if I could have access to my room. Considering that it was about 11.30 am and check-in time was at 3.00 pm, my chances of getting into my room were slim, but luck was on my side and I was given my key. Once in my room I pulled Cardboard Paul out of the suitcase and laid him on the chair to stretch him out after the long flight.

The hotel room was a decent-size twin bedroom and had a good view of the palm trees, buildings and roadways – I could see clearly that I was now in the big city. I unpacked my toiletries and some clothes and headed into the shower to freshen up and keep me going for a few more hours.

Feeling refreshed after my shower and dressed in my summer gear, I was starving. I went downstairs and asked the porter where I could go to find some food. He gave me directions to the main street of downtown LA.

With a hat on my head to shield me from the heat and sun, I proceeded to explore the city. All the roads and streets were one-way and the traffic was hectic and very noisy. It was a concrete jungle – busy and frantic with cars tooting their horns liberally, and sirens from emergency vehicles was a constant noise. It reminded me of Sydney, although much larger and more intense.

1. Our Journey Begins

I was walking down the main street with a smile on my face and a street vendor said hello to me. Of course, I said hello back. He then immediately asked, 'Where are you from? Are you English?'

I laughed and said, 'No, I'm Australian.'

He smiled and said, 'Welcome!' Ah, there it was, the first moment I felt somewhat welcomed into this country.

I walked a bit further down the street and found Target Centre that had a food court in the basement where I could sit down and eat.

Walking along the streets, there were many differences compared to what I was used to. Vehicles are left-hand drive and drive on the opposite side of the road, which was very confusing. I was checking both ways constantly when crossing the road. The traffic lights had a tiny human figure walking and then would display how many seconds were left to cross the road.

I spotted three MINI cars, which was a sign from Paul letting me know that he was around. It wouldn't be the only time as I continually saw MINIs on my journey around the USA and it became a standing joke of how many we could spot.

After eating, I wandered back to the hotel and went up to my room. I lied down on the bed for a rest and, before I knew it, I had dozed off for a few hours. It was much needed as I had been awake for over twenty-four hours and felt tired and very dizzy. The tour guide, Judy, called on the hotel phone, welcomed me and gave me some tips on where to shop and buy food. She also advised that she would be at the hotel reception the next day after 3.00 pm and asked me to come by and say hello.

I looked over the tourist brochures and guides to see what I could do the next day. I still had to find a place to get a sim card and sort out my mobile data whilst I was in the USA.

I wandered back into Target Centre to find supplies as well as some melatonin which my naturopath suggested to help with jet lag. I found a large bottle of melatonin and water. I also needed a coffee so I ordered one from a Starbucks on my way out. Target Centre was huge and had everything that you ever wanted – a one-stop shop.

It was my first night in LA and I decided to have dinner in the hotel restaurant. Although somewhat expensive, dinner was delicious and well worth the price. By the end of the night, I had already met some ladies from our tour and organised to meet up with one of them, Lynda, for breakfast the next morning.

By the time I got back to my room I was really exhausted, so I took a dose of melatonin, set the alarm and fell asleep as soon as my head hit the pillow.

Cardboard Paul was still stretched out on the chair when I woke up. I decided to pack him away as I knew that sometime that day another tour member – my room buddy – was going to join me and I didn't want to give her a shock when she came into the room.

I met Lynda downstairs in the restaurant for breakfast and we chatted away about our lives, where we were from, what we were looking forward to on this tour, and so much more. After breakfast, we said goodbye as we both had planned different activities for the day.

I planned to go to Universal Studios for the day and asked the porter for the best and cheapest way to get there. He suggested taking the train as a taxi to and from Universal Studios would cost about USD$80. So, I decided to take a stroll back into town to take the train.

Along the way, I went to the local telecommunications shop to sort out my mobile data. I went into the T-Mobile shop and was greeted by lovely shop assistants who organised a 30-day plan for me and put a new sim card in my phone. We chatted about where I was from and I told them that I was travelling with Cardboard Paul. They laughed and thought it amazing that I was honouring Paul that way.

1. Our Journey Begins

I wandered to the next block and down to the metro station. The tickets were cheap and easy to purchase. I easily found the platform to catch the train. Whilst I was waiting, I saw Maria from our tour and asked her what she was doing for the day. Maria was in two minds as to what she was doing but decided to tag along with me to Universal Studios. Our train finally arrived and after about twenty minutes, we arrived at our destination and found where we needed to go to catch the bus to Universal Studios.

Universal Studios was massive and there were people everywhere. It was a beautiful, hot and sunny day with huge crowds waiting to get in. We found where we needed to be, paid for our tickets and walked through the big gates. With a map in hand, we roamed through the different streets and headed towards the Harry Potter section. My daughter, Sarah, wanted me to buy a Harry Potter magic wand for her. It wasn't difficult finding one as there were plenty of options, but there were so many different types of wands for the different Harry Potter characters and I wasn't sure which character she wanted. I had to text Sarah asking her what she wanted and due to the time difference, I had to wait a while to get the answer.

There was so much to do and see. We jumped on the Universal Studios tour to look at the back lots and had shark jaws jump out at us, although it wasn't as scary, unlike the film. It was fascinating to look at all the different areas and sections where movies are filmed. My favourite was going through the King Kong section which was in 3-D and had dinosaurs. Kong himself came at us from all angles that was scary but thrilling at the same time.

When we finished the tour, we decided to get lunch. Maria and I each bought a turkey sandwich which was huge and came with chips on the side – though they were not my usual version of hot potato chips but potato crisps instead.

After a quick feed, we headed to the Harry Potter castle and queued for over an hour to go through this massive castle that led to some scary rides that neither of us wanted to go on. As it was so hot, every now and then there would be a sprinkler providing a cool place to stand. I was so glad that I wore my sunhat.

After having a good look around the castle, we headed towards the Minions ride which I mistakenly thought would have been more sedated. This was a 3-D ride where you sat down in front of a big screen. You really feel as though you are flying through the air and falling as the seats move with you, it's very realistic.

By this time, I had heard from Sarah on which wand she wanted and, of course, it was Harry Potter's wand. I headed towards one of the stores that sold Harry Potter merchandise and purchased the wand for her. On our way out, Maria wanted to try the infamous Butter Beer that was being sold out of wooden carts designed to look like they came straight from the Harry Potter world. Maria tasted the beer and said it wasn't too bad, I didn't want to try it as it looked sickly.

The final attraction we wanted to see was the Water World show. When we arrived at the show area, the queue was already incredibly long. Maria, in her wisdom, went to the front of the queue and asked the attendant when the show was going to start, we then just milled around the area ahead of the queue – very sneaky. This show was spectacular – and wet, if you sat in the front row seats. It was fun, entertaining and thrilling. Plenty of photo opportunities, and I also took videos of most of the action.

After a long day, we headed towards the exit gates and boarded the bus that took us back to the train station. I was tired and hot, and my feet were hurting from all the walking we had done.

Once back at the hotel our tour guide, Judy, was in residence where she had said she would be. I wandered up to the room to have a quick refresh and arrived to a dark room with my room buddy fast asleep in bed. Not wanting to disturb her, I went to the bathroom and quickly headed downstairs to talk to Judy and find out what was happening the next day when our tour started. After chatting with Judy, I caught up with some other ladies that were on our tour and made arrangements to catch up for drinks and snacks at the hotel bar.

I wandered back up to the room and my buddy woke up. I apologised for waking her. I introduced myself and she introduced herself

1. Our Journey Begins

as Pauline. I asked if she wanted to come down for drinks but she declined as she had come in early that day from Perth and wanted to catch up on her sleep. I wished her a good night's sleep and told her we would talk more in the morning.

I went back downstairs to the bar to catch up with my fellow travellers. After a few drinks and some things to eat, I went back to my room and Pauline woke up again. We introduced ourselves again and spoke briefly on where we were from and our backgrounds. I also introduced Cardboard Paul to Pauline who thought it was amazing that I was travelling with him, honouring his memory and travelling solo. It was interesting to hear that Pauline was also a widow who had lost her husband over twenty years ago. After our quick catch-up it was time for me to get into bed for a well-earned sleep, I was exhausted but also excited.

2
Los Angeles

Day 2 – Los Angeles City Highlights

The first day of the tour had finally arrived, Pauline and I were up early as we had to meet the rest of our tour buddies and board the bus by 8.30 am for the Los Angeles city highlights tour.

I left Cardboard Paul in the room as I didn't think it was a good idea to introduce him too early on in our tour, so he just laid packed in my suitcase – I also didn't want to scare the cleaning staff.

Pauline and I went downstairs, met some familiar faces and lined up to get on the bus. Judy had allocated seats using post-it notes stuck above the seats on the overhead luggage locker. Pauline and I found our seats and were happy to find out we were seat buddies. At first, we were a little confused as we were not sure if we were going to be swapped or moved. Judy then explained the seat rotation procedure – our assigned seats changed every day to ensure that we had a different view but also the opportunity to talk with other people as we rotated. We were in luck as our seats were rotated together in pairs throughout the tour. We shared rooms and sat together on the bus, we were both relieved and happy.

The bus was pretty full with 49 passengers excluding Judy and our bus driver, Piroshka. Our tour consisted of mostly Australians; 32 Aussies, 3 from Wales, 2 pair of couples from Auckland, New Zealand and 10 from the United Kingdom – consisting of families, couples, friends and a mother and son duo.

We had six single females and two single males that were paired up with each other. I was very fortunate to be paired with Pauline. I don't believe this was a chance meeting – Pauline and I were meant to meet and share a room.

We were off and the chatter and excitement in the bus was noticeable as we were all very excited to start our tour. Judy, on her microphone, started pointing out buildings and areas of interest. We were heading towards the Chinese Theatre, famous for the handprints and footprints of stars at its forecourt.

I noticed that people in LA were very laid back and friendly, the city was also relatively clean. When we were near the Chinese Theatre, it was crowded and filled with people dressed up as movie characters that wanted to take a photo with you – and they wanted you to pay them in exchange for these photos, of course. There were also people offering passers-by to pet their large albino pythons. I certainly stayed clear of those. Although we walked past them so many times, each time I walked quickly and as far away as possible. Pauline made sure she was between me and the snakes, it was very funny and scary all at the same time. Pauline became my big protector when it came to the snakes.

We had a good wander around and Judy brought us into the Paramount Centre that had a perfect view of the Hollywood sign. We had some free time, so Pauline and I found a kiosk that was selling magnets, hats, glasses and T-shirts. I purchased my first souvenir – a baseball cap and red T-shirt. I had left my sunhat in the hotel room which was not smart. I had to find some kind of hat to wear whilst we were walking around under the sun and heat. It was very hot in LA and I needed to keep cool as much as I could. Pauline bought some magnets to start off her collection on this tour.

We also booked a tour around the Hollywood Hills that promised to show us where the stars lived. With the Hollywood Hills tour, tickets for Madame Tussauds wax museum was included, so Pauline and I lined up and wandered around the different displays, taking plenty of photos beside our favourite stars. Some of the wax figures were life-like and others just bore average resemblance to its celebrity. We had so much fun and laughed like we hadn't laughed in a long time.

Our time slot for the Hollywood Hills tour arrived and we bundled into the back of an open vehicle. I was very relieved that I had bought the cap as it was very sunny and hot in the back of the vehicle. Our tour guide welcomed us all and proceeded to drive towards the Hills.

2. Los Angeles

Whilst driving through the Hills and being shown all the different stars' homes, the views of the Hills and the Hollywood sign were surreal. I pinched myself and said to Pauline, 'Wow, we are in LA, can you believe this?'

There were plenty of photo opportunities and I went crazy photographing the views, the Hills and the celebrity homes that I found interesting. We saw a lot of gates and roofs and felt it was worth driving around the Hills, but we didn't know if the actual stars lived in the homes that the tour guide pointed out. Despite that, there were some spectacular and expensive homes and I imagine you would have to be a multi-millionaire to be able to afford a house in the area. I was interested in Audrey Hepburn's home and took a photo of that and sent it to my sister who is a huge fan.

On our way back to the Chinese Theatre, we drove down Rodeo Drive which, again, was unreal. All the comments about Julia Roberts and *Pretty Woman* was mentioned, including the classic line, 'Big mistake, big, huge. I have to go shopping now.'

We finally arrived back at our destination and had another wander around the shops near the Chinese Theatre. I bought some thongs which were very welcomed as I had packed limited footwear and just needed something to slip on. Pauline found some more magnets and we left the shop very happy customers.

As our tour bus had already departed for the day, we had to find our own way home. We went to the nearest metro station and caught a train back to the hotel. I found the metro really easy and cheap, plus it wasn't as scary as we thought it would be. After getting off at our station, we walked across the road to the Target shopping centre and found this great little Greek food place downstairs where you could dine in or take away. We decided to sit down and eat and met up with some of the other Aussies that were on our tour.

After dinner, we wandered back to our hotel and started preparing for the next day's tour that will take us out of Los Angeles. The day before, Judy had given us our itinerary advising us where we were staying, what time we had to have our suitcases ready for collection, what time was breakfast, and the time to get on the bus. It was very fortunate that Pauline and I were extremely organised. We had our clothes prepared and bags packed effortlessly before we went to sleep. We sat up in bed watching a bit of television and chatted about what was ahead of us. We were very excited, like little school girls going on this big adventure.

Day 3 – Los Angeles – Palm Springs – Scottsdale

We had set both our alarms for 6.00 am to ensure we didn't sleep in, although we were both too excited for that to happen. Our bags had to be ready at 6.45 am and we were departing at 7.45 am. Pauline was first to wake up and shower, she was so quick I was amazed. I had my shower, which took much longer than Pauline's. Our bags were ready by the time the porter knocked on the door at 6.45 am and we made our way downstairs to the lobby around 7.30 am.

Everyone gathered together and the excitement in the air could be measured by the noise levels as everyone was hanging around and chatting. We all lined up ready to get on the bus and as we found our seats, we sat and waited in anticipation as Piroshka and Judy were last to board. We took off and said farewell to LA.

I had packed Cardboard Paul in his calico bag and placed him up in the overhead luggage compartment, safe and sound ready to be taken out when we arrived at our first destination, Palm Springs – a desert oasis with its distinctive wind farms, 5,000 swimming pools and 90 golf courses. We didn't have breakfast yet but were promised something to eat once we reached there. Palm Springs was about an hour and a half out from LA and I was starting to feel really hungry by then.

The bus was parked at the back of a little shopping strip, and as we climbed off the bus the heat hit us hard. It was a very dry heat and we were sweating before we even stepped foot on the ground. We wandered into town to find the nearest café to have breakfast. Everyone seemed

2. Los Angeles

to make a beeline to Ruby's Diner which was like stepping back into the 50's with all its cool vintage furniture and red, white and blue Americana everywhere. We grabbed a table and took turns to go to the restrooms whilst the others studied the menu. I ordered cinnamon roll French toast and Pauline ordered eggs benedict. We also shared a serving of beignets which were like small donuts without the holes that were served hot and you dipped them into a strawberry flavoured yoghurt. I washed them down with a nice cup of tea – I didn't trust the coffee. The Americans are huge coffee drinkers, so their choice of teas were very limited.

When the bill arrived, Pauline and I were still trying to get used to the American tipping etiquette and was totally confused by it. To make matters worse, we had issues differentiating American money. We split the bill and put down what we thought was enough. We both wandered out of the restaurant and within a few minutes we were being chased down by one of the dining staff letting us know that we didn't pay enough money. We both apologised profusely and gave them the balance of money owed. Both Pauline and I shook our heads and laughed so much, but this wasn't the end of our total confusion over American money.

After our embarrassing blunder, we walked over to the centre of town where a statue of Sonny Bono was sitting on the edge of a water fountain. Sonny had been Mayor of Palms Springs, but he was also famously known as the ex-husband of singer Cher. We saw this as a photo opportunity and Cardboard Paul was pulled from his calico bag for a great photo of us together with Sonny. We had some weird looks from people wandering past, but I just smiled.

After our rest and feed, we were back on the bus for our next destination, Scottsdale. We were driving past the arid desert and was feeling the heat, despite the bus being nicely air-conditioned. Pauline and I were still laughing about our little mishap at Ruby's Diner and told our fellow passengers about the ordeal.

As we were driving through the desert, I was taking plenty of photos and updating Facebook whilst we had internet coverage. The Wi-Fi on the bus was a hit and miss and my phone coverage was also in and out. We were often out of phone range and jumped between different phone carriers.

The long ride to Scottsdale gave us all an opportunity to get to know each other more. Judy suggested that each of us stand up and say a little something about ourselves for five minutes in front of the group. It was fascinating to hear everyone's stories. It was my turn and I told the group about my story with Paul and how I made a promise to take him travelling with me – so that's why they will see the cardboard cut-out of Paul – and how I was writing a book about my experience. At this time, I didn't have a title for the book yet but knew I was writing one. The title of the book was yet to come to me and much sooner than I thought!

We finally arrived at our accommodation for the night at Scottsdale, the Holiday Inn. It was very roomy and comfortable with a separate lounge. Pauline and I chose our beds – I was usually next to the window as Pauline wanted to be away from the sunlight.

We were up for a treat for our dinner at Rustler's Rooste – a country and western themed restaurant in the hills. I packed Cardboard Paul in the calico bag and saw it as an opportunity to take him out for dinner and dancing with plenty of photo opportunities.

As we arrived for dinner, it was explained to us that we could enter the restaurant through a slide or a door. Pauline and I looked at each other, laughed and agreed that there was no way we were going down a slide! Some of our tour buddies decided to take the plunge and went down the long slide, it was very funny.

We were escorted into a large room with very long tables and sat down with the rest of our tour group. We were offered beer, wine and soft drinks, and there were big bowls of salad and bread on the table.

I said to Pauline, 'Let's take some photos of Cardboard Paul on the dance floor, near some big barrels and the cardboard cut-out of Kenny Chesney.'

The salad was taken off the table and our mains were served. I was a little disappointed as I wanted to add salad to my meal but I found out that Americans usually have their salads separately as an entree. The meal was delicious and was completed with candy floss on a stick for dessert. The night was over, and we headed back to our hotel room for some well-earned sleep as we had to be up at 6.00 am for our bags to be collected at 6.30 am. As always, Pauline and I were packed and ready before bedtime. Our next stop was Flagstaff, Arizona to see the Grand Canyon.

Day 4 – Scottsdale to Flagstaff

Our alarm went off at 6.00 am and we had our luggage ready for the 6.30 am collection. Breakfast was a hit and miss with the eggs being rubbery and watery, so I had a banana just to curb my hunger.

At 7.30 am, our bus took us on our big adventure to the Grand Canyon. Pauline and I were chatting away and connected with new tour buddies as we moved from one side of the bus to the other as part of the seat rotation. We had only known each other for a few days, but it was as if Pauline and I had been lifelong friends. When the others asked how long we had been friends, we both laughed and admitted that we had only met a few days ago.

We were back on the bus and were travelling through some spectacular scenery, through mountains and desert, seeing the odd wind farms with massive wind turbines turning slowly in the middle of the desert. Heading towards our first stop, Sedona – a thriving centre for New Age arts – was exciting and right up my alley. I looked forward to exploring this part of the country. The mountains that surrounded this oasis were spectacular with the rich brownness in the mountains and different levels of colour from centuries gone by.

Our tour bus arrived at Sedona and we piled off the bus ready to explore this amazing town. The energy here was electric and I could feel the calmness surrounding me. I grabbed Cardboard Paul, then Pauline and I proceeded to walk around the area and take photographs. We were very fortunate to find some great props in the street that we could take photos with. There was a huge statue of a horse where Cardboard Paul and I stood under – we were dwarfed by the size of this statue. As my trusty photographer Pauline snapped away, Cardboard Paul and I stood smiling and watched the weird looks we were getting from people passing by.

We wandered further up the street and found a wooden Native American sculpture outside a souvenir shop called Rollies Camera (since 1961). A brass plaque on the wall explained the history of the store. It was originally Bob Bradshaw's photo shop and living quarters from 1948. His photos often appeared on the Arizona Highways and he even published several books featuring images of Arizona. Bob was also involved in Arizona's film making business for 50 years. He even sold horse rides from stables behind the studio / shop. Rollie Houck then bought the shop in 1961.

We had another photo opportunity with a life-size dummy dressed as a cowboy complete with jeans, jacket, scarf, cowboy boots and hat. On the shop window, a sign showed 'Wanted: Arizona Rangers' – we were in real cowboy country now.

After taking our photos, I packed Cardboard Paul back into his calico bag. Pauline and I wandered the streets, peering through all the windows and wandering into the many shops that had New Age goodies and jewellery.

One of the shops was selling different types of donuts. I have never seen anything like it, they looked amazing and yummy. Both of us didn't dare walk into the shop; I could feel the weight piling on just looking at these moreish sweets.

Judy told us about a great little coffee shop that sold some really delicious rolls and sandwiches. We walked towards a little arcade and two Arizona rangers were standing on the footpath. As we passed them, we said 'G'day' and asked for directions to this little coffee shop. After striking up a quick chat, we followed their directions, walked up the arcade to the next street and found the café. The menu was minimal but we both found something nourishing to eat. Both Pauline and I bought a chicken salad roll which was delicious. In hindsight, we could have bought one roll and shared between the two of us as the servings were huge.

We wandered back to where the bus was parked and, after having a quick toilet break, we clambered up the steps back into our seats. I placed Cardboard Paul back up in his usual position in the overhead compartment where he safely remained until our next stop. I was still getting used to entering the bus from the right hand side, I would often walk to the driver's side first before realising the passenger entrance was on the other side. I wasn't the only Aussie that had done this.

We were back on the road, passing through the weather-sculpted rock formations of the stunning Oak Creek Canyon, the Mogollon Rim, the San Francisco Peaks, and finally arriving at our destination – one of the natural wonders of the world – the Grand Canyon. Before reaching the park, we dropped off a few brave souls that were booked into the optional helicopter flightseeing excursion. Although the experience and views would have been spectacular, Pauline and I did not even contemplate getting into a helicopter and firmly decided to keep our feet on the ground.

After dropping off the helicopter passengers, we meandered through winding roads and spectacular scenery with red mountain rocks of different shades, showing the different ages that these magnificent mountains have stood the test of time, with tall, green pine tree forests splattered in between.

The bus dropped us off at the entrance of the Grand Canyon, but the view of the canyon itself was blocked by all the buildings in front of it. I grabbed Cardboard Paul from the overhead locker and tucked him under my arm.

It wasn't until we went through the doors and out onto the canyon rim itself that the breathtaking expansion and energy of the canyon was felt. It just took my breath away, tears rolled down my eyes as I

Travelling With Cardboard Paul

paused for a moment to experience the energy and be in the moment. This was a special moment in a sacred space and I was happy to share it with Cardboard Paul and Pauline. It was spectacular, as Paul would have said.

We wandered around the canyon rim, being careful not to get too close to the edge, and found a great spot for our photo opportunity with Cardboard Paul. As I posed with him and my ever-trusty photographer Pauline was snapping away, I could see the looks and glances coming our way. People were staring at us and wondering what we were doing. By this time, I had become very comfortable with taking photos with Cardboard Paul and found it amusing.

A lady was sitting on one of the bench seats eating ice cream on a cone, she watched us and eventually asked what was the significance of the cut-out. I told her the story of how I was travelling around the world with him and writing a book about our travels. I told her that the book was called 'Travelling with Cardboard Paul'. In that moment, the title just came to me and it was the first time I said it. Pauline and I laughed and thought it was a great title for a book. The lady laughed and said that I made her day, aside from the visit to the Grand Canyon. She thought I was brave and expressed her love for the title of the book. Before we went our separate ways, she said she was sorry for my loss and wished me well.

Pauline and I continued our tour around the canyon and wandered into Hopi House – a Native American arts and crafts historical landmark. There was a photo opportunity at the front of this beautiful rich brownstone building, and across the road in a patch of green grass, two deer's were grazing – another photo opportunity. We refrained from buying any arts and crafts and returned back towards the visitor's centre looking for something to eat.

On our way back we stopped at the El Tovar Hotel which had a huge veranda with wooden cane chairs for the guests to sit on – another photo opportunity. I sat Cardboard Paul on the chair and stood behind him whilst Pauline clicked away.

2. Los Angeles

Again, I packed up Cardboard Paul into his calico bag and we walked back to the visitor's centre looking for food. We found a restaurant along a hallway and asked for a table. The young girl at the entrance may have been confused by our accent and – perhaps without understanding what we were asking for – turned us away. Pauline and I were not too happy about this, so we walked away and looked for somewhere else to eat. We couldn't find any other suitable place, so we walked right back to the restaurant and were fortunate that another person was greeting customers at the door.

We had a lovely young man who was our server. After perusing the menu, we both decided on the cheesecake and coffee. Taking our first bite, we both felt like we were in cheesecake heaven. Neither of us had tasted anything like this before, it was light, not too sweet and had strawberries on top, glazed in a delicate light sauce. I have had a cheesecake or two over the years, but nothing compared to this.

After having our afternoon tea, we wandered into the gift shop – not a good idea! Pauline and I went crazy in the shop, buying up some really nice souvenirs for the family and, of course, for ourselves. I found these gorgeous earrings that reflected the colours of the Grand Canyon. After purchasing them, I put them on straightaway and didn't take them off until I arrived back home. Everyone commented on these earrings and I still receive compliments whenever I wear them. After maxing out both our credit cards, we had a quick toilet break and headed back to the bus for our next port of call, Flagstaff.

Back on the bus, I tucked Cardboard Paul back in the overhead locker and started chatting with our fellow passengers on their experience, and especially on what they bought. We had two lovely ladies, Kris and Dianne, two friends from Sydney that really loved to shop. We were always interested to hear and see what they had bought.

We headed to our next motel in Flagstaff, driving through the magnificent mountains and forest while gaining altitude. After arriving, while making our way towards our rooms via the elevator, we could see an indoor pool just waiting for us to slide in and swim. Pauline and I threw our suitcases on the bed and unpacked our bathers to swim after dinner.

We had a quick change into something other than our travelling dresses for our evening meal. We headed for the hotel restaurant and sat in a booth with Lynda and Margo, sharing our stories and highlights of the day.

After dinner, Pauline and I headed back to the room for another quick change into our bathers, grabbed a towel and headed for the pool with the water so blue, warm and inviting. We stayed in the pool for a few hours and finished the night off by relaxing in the spa. We were the only two people left in the pool for a while until another man entered the pool, stepped into the spa for a short time and then left. We finally eased ourselves away from the pool, having a quick shower before packing for the next day and jumping into bed.

That night I had the weirdest dreams I have ever had in all my life! There was a valid reason for this, and I wasn't the only one.

3
Las Vegas

Day 5 – Flagstaff to Las Vegas

We had another early morning with bags having to be ready at 6.30 am, so Pauline and I were prepared from the previous night. Pauline was in the shower first and was out within a few seconds. I've never seen anyone shower as quickly as her. I told Pauline about my weird dreams and she mentioned that she had some crazy ones as well.

We had our breakfast downstairs at 7.00 am and the food was another hit and miss. I grabbed whatever edible food was available and headed towards the bus for our 7.30 am departure. As soon as I got to the bus, I started feeling really sick and felt like I was going to pass out. I made a dash for the closest toilet, although not vomiting, I did not feel good. Once my stomach settled, I mentioned to Pauline that I was feeling unwell and she offered me a Stemetil from her stash for travel sickness. Apparently, weird dreams and feeling sick and dizzy goes with the high altitude that we were in – 2,106 metres above sea level. As I was extremely sensitive to anything and everything, it hit me pretty hard.

The bus was packed with our luggage and everyone piled on again for our next journey to Las Vegas. We found our new seats for the day and were working our way closer towards the front of the bus. We had been travelling for about half an hour and Judy started passing out carrier bags which had the picture of the Grand Canyon on the side. Pauline and I started calling it our Judy bag and it came in hand throughout all my travels when I need a bag big enough to put some items – especially if I was swimming in the hotel pool or heading into the local shop for some supplies.

Upon leaving the mountain town of Flagstaff, we travelled on historic Route 66 and crossed the old Mojave gold strike county which bore traces of century-old ghost towns set in the natural beauty of the desert. The song *(Get Your Kicks On) Route 66* was stuck in my head.

We had been travelling for a while and Judy was describing to us the history of Route 66, how it was rejuvenated and put back on the map by Angel Delgadillo – dubbed the 'guardian angel' of US Route 66. He is the main founder of the Historic Route 66 Association of Arizona, established in 1987 to campaign for the 'Historic Route 66' signage on the former US highway.

We were excited to visit Seligman, Arizona and see his shop, Angel & Vilma's Route 66 Gift Shop. Angel, being a barber, was often seen at the shop despite no longer being a spring chicken at ninety years of age. We were very fortunate to meet him in person and have our photos taken with him on the old-fashioned barber chair. Although I left Cardboard Paul in the bus, there were plenty of photo opportunities with other cardboard cut-outs – I hope Cardboard Paul will never find out. The shop was full of awesome gifts and souvenirs. I bought a red number plate with Route 66 on it, among other cool little items.

After our quick contact with the famous, we went across the road to another shop to buy lunch to have on the bus. It was time again to climb up into the bus and take our seats for the next stage of our journey – Las Vegas. You could feel the excitement and energy in the bus and I even started singing *Viva Las Vegas* Elvis style.

We were travelling along the highway through the vast desert and awesome mountains that surrounded us in the distance. Judy was updating us with all the highlights of Las Vegas and even passed around a handout, 'Judy's Las Vegas Favourites', which included maps, shopping and transport information. Judy also highlighted other tourist spots to visit whilst in town, including the Mob Museum and the many classic cars museums. I already knew which one of those two Pauline and I were going to explore.

All of a sudden, the desert we were driving through turned into suburbia. We had arrived in Las Vegas with the big sign 'Welcome to Las Vegas' in full view as we made our way down the main strip. The enormous casinos towering over us from both sides of the strip was a sight to see. Both sides of the Las Vegas Boulevard had huge casinos trying to outdo one another, each one with their unique theme. There were statues and buildings depicting New York City and Paris, we drove past famous casinos such as the Bellagio and Caesars Palace, to name a few, and then there were the singing fountains, waterfalls and so much more.

We finally arrived at our accommodation for the next few nights, Harrah's Las Vegas Hotel and Casino. The bus parked underground and as we stepped off, the heat and humidity hit us like a wave – or more like a tsunami. It was extremely hot and we had been very comfortable in the air-conditioned bus. We grabbed our luggage from Piroshka and proceeded to the check-in counter of the hotel.

As we walked into the very cool, air-conditioned foyer, we could smell the perfume in the air. Apparently, there is a particular smell that casinos have perfected to keep people inside so they spend more money. Judy had already gone ahead to organise our keys and once we had ours, we were off to our rooms to refresh, change and explore the hotel.

Pauline and I arrived at our hotel room and the door was wide open. We peered in and saw a housekeeper sitting on the chair looking at her phone whilst talking to another in the bathroom. I think we really surprised them as we asked if our room was ready since we were already given the keys. One of them said, 'Oh no, we are waiting for our manager to let us know what is going on.' They eventually left and we had our room but this was just the beginning of the poor service at this hotel.

We finally unpacked our bags and changed to head downstairs to explore the hotel. I left Cardboard Paul in his calico bag on the bed just to chill out whilst we were out. We wandered downstairs where the hotel lobby had plenty of interesting shops and restaurants. There were slot machines and tables everywhere and security at every door. We wandered around the ground floor getting our bearings and found a place to sit down and have coffee. Although we didn't have too much time to explore, we found the closest Starbucks and sat down to have a well-earned coffee before heading up to our room again to get ready for the evening.

Travelling With Cardboard Paul

As these three days would be spent at our leisure, there were optional tours and entertainment that we could see. We had booked a restaurant and a Las Vegas show for the evening with a stop at Fremont Street afterwards. They say this city never sleeps and it really doesn't; there is always something going on and there are people everywhere.

I had looked up the entertainment happening in Las Vegas during our stay and found that Rod Stewart was playing at The Colosseum at Caesars Palace on the same night we arrived. Unfortunately, as timing was really tight, I couldn't line up the event with our timing. If he had been performing on the following evening, I would have definitely booked tickets to see him.

After getting dressed, Pauline and I headed down to the car park to board the bus for our night out on the town.

We were settled in our seats and Judy asked if I had Cardboard Paul on board. I answered no and asked why. She went on to explain that she had asked the organiser of the event at Planet Hollywood for our dinner and the show if we could bring Cardboard Paul with us. The organiser said he wasn't sure what to say as they have never had a request like that before. Unfortunately, the show was full so they didn't have a spare seat for Cardboard Paul. I laughed as much as the rest of the crew on the bus, it was hilarious and even more so if I had taken Cardboard Paul out for the night. Cardboard Paul was becoming his own entity with his own personality. Paul would have thought it was hysterical and wouldn't believe that I was doing such a thing.

We went for our dinner at a nice restaurant in Planet Hollywood filled with plenty of food, drinks and laughter. The room was packed and extremely loud, but we still had a great evening. After dinner, it was time to head into the venue for the Las Vegas show. Pauline and I noted that there were other shows happening as well. As we had a few free days to explore, we kept it in the back of our minds.

The Las Vegas show was fun and entertaining and portrayed the evolution of Las Vegas from the 40's up until the current times. It paid homage to legends that helped coin Las Vegas as the Entertainment

3. Las Vegas

Capital of the World. From the Rat Pack to Elvis to Tina Turner, and also portrayed the classic and timeless glamour that rang true to a Las Vegas show.

After the show, we walked back to the bus where Piroshka was waiting for us. We were driven down to the famous Fremont Street Experience and dropped off at Binion's Casino to get a photo with a million dollars. Pauline was really looking forward to Fremont Street as she had heard how great it was. Fremont Street was not your average street but a seven block entertainment district with the world's largest video screen providing free light shows every night of the week. It also provided live concerts and entertainment on three stages, as well as different entertainers throughout the centre.

Arriving at Fremont Street, we could not believe our eyes. There were two men playing music that were practically butt naked and young women scantily dressed with their breasts hanging out – we didn't know where to look. In the end, Pauline and I were just laughing while picking out the best and worst sights. There were people everywhere and it was extremely noisy with people in your face trying to sell you something. Pauline and I hurried down to the end of the street, having had enough. Pauline felt really disappointed as the experience did not live up to her expectation.

I bet Cardboard Paul and I could have set up in the middle of the street and charged people to have photos with him. I am sure we would have made a few bucks and Paul would have thought it was funny. We then wandered over to another casino that had a huge swimming pool in the centre surrounded by this magnificent indoor aquarium, it was amazing.

Finally, we were back on the bus and, after doing some more touring around Vegas, we headed back to the casino for the night. Considering we were not too sleepy and could sleep in the next morning, we decided to have a nightcap downstairs. Pauline found this quiet little spot where you could play different types of Keno and I grabbed us some coffee from Starbucks. We sat down and played a few rounds whilst sipping on our coffees.

After losing our money, we went upstairs to our rooms for a well-earned rest. It had been a very long day and the next few days were planned for exploring and shows, with shopping being on top of the list.

We put the television on and the news that Hurricane Harvey was bearing down on Houston started to become a concern as I was heading towards Houston in two weeks' time.

As soon as my head hit the pillow, I was sound asleep. I think the clock read 1.30 am and the alarm was set for 9 am.

Day 6 – Las Vegas Casino and Beatles Show

We were awake and Pauline was first in the shower again. I went into the bathroom after her to wake up and freshen up. We were dressed and headed downstairs for breakfast.

The restaurant in the casino looked good. We took our seats and were shortly greeted by a very friendly waitress, Miss Vanessa, who gave us a menu and proceeded to pour some tea for me and coffee for Pauline whilst we perused the menu.

Pauline and I shared French toast with scrambled eggs and bacon after Miss Vanessa pointed out that the French toast had six pieces of toast per serving. It would be better to share that and choose another side dish. It was delicious and one of the better breakfasts I had since the beginning of the tour. We tipped our waitress generously and wandered out into the sunlight and heat on the strip for some serious exploring.

We wandered over to the casino that had the theme of Paris. Everything was huge, it was hot and humid, and the footpaths were crowded and busy. Again, someone was always in your face trying to sell you something. We entered the casino and found this lovely little café. Pauline and I ordered coffee and shared a large ham and brie cheese baguette. The baguette was delicious and moreish and we both totally loved it.

As we sat eating our lunch in this Parisienne setting, we started discussing what we wanted to do that afternoon, evening and the next day. We knew that we wanted to see more shows and do some serious shopping. We decided to hit the shops; the Fashion Show Mall was just down the road. If anyone has been to Las Vegas, they will know that everything there is huge, especially the distance between the blocks as the casinos take up one block which can cover miles and miles. We decided that it was too far to walk and also extremely hot and humid, so we decided to take the bus – that was an adventure in itself.

We asked the attendant near the bus stop how and where to buy tickets and they showed us where to go. Tickets in hand, we waited for the bus to arrive. Whilst waiting, Pauline and I were just chatting away with each other and the guy sitting next to us asked, 'Are you from Australia?'

We said, 'Yes.' He then proceeded to go on about how dangerous it was in Australia with all the snakes and spiders that killed you and how wonderful Steve Irwin was. Pauline and I just looked at each other and laughed and explained to the man that you don't need to believe everything you hear and that it was not that dangerous in Australia.

Our bus finally arrived. After two stops, we got off and walked over one of the huge overpasses to get to the shopping centre. Once inside the centre, it was cool and welcomed as the sweat was pouring off me, which says a lot since I am not one to sweat that much. We found a seat in the huge food court and skulled down an ice-cold drink, it was very refreshing. We wandered through a few shops and found this cool shop that sold bags and jewellery. I bought a few items and so did Pauline.

Next stop was the Sketchers store which sold really cheap shoes including styles that weren't available in Australia. Pauline had trouble with her shoes and I suggested for her to buy a pair of Sketchers as they were comfortable. I assured her that she wouldn't regret it. After choosing two pairs of shoes each, we both walked out of the shop very happy customers.

We had finished shopping and my credit card felt better for it, although it was getting a bit anorexic due to the amount of money I was spending. We decided to take the bus back, but it took us well past our hotel and we ended up walking back in the heat. It was not clever as it was extremely hot and humid. Once back at the hotel, we asked the concierge for tickets to the Beatles show that evening at Planet Hollywood and Human Nature show at the Venetian the following evening.

With our tickets in hand we went back up to the room to get ready for the Beatles show. Once dressed, we headed downstairs and slowly walked to Planet Hollywood which was just a block or two away. We explored all the shops in Planet Hollywood before heading to the show.

Pauline and I absolutely loved the music and the band. The show followed the Beatles from the very beginning until their last concert. The performers resembled closely the famous four Beatles and sounded pretty close too. After the concert, we continued walking around Planet Hollywood before heading back to our hotel for a night cap – which was a Starbucks coffee and Keno at the hotel bar.

It didn't feel like it, but it was already 2 am by the time we went back to our room. Time stood still in the casino because there were no clocks to be found aside from your personal watches or phones – you wouldn't know if it was day or night outside.

As we got back to the room, I switched on the television and the news was all about how devastating Hurricane Harvey was on Houston. I started to become really concerned as my whole Texas tour was on the line and I had to think of plan B if I couldn't stay in Houston.

Day 7 – Las Vegas Car Museum and Human Nature Show

*A*s we had another free day in Vegas, Pauline and I had a long sleep in and woke up around 10 am. We went back down for breakfast and were very disappointed that the lovely Miss Vanessa wasn't working that morning. The lady that served us was neither happy nor helpful and I don't think she spoke much English either, as she became very confused over the cups of coffee and walked away after showing us our table.

Another lady came over and took our order. We ordered the same French toast with scrambled eggs and bacon from the previous day. Again, the food was delicious and, by this time, we had the American money – especially the tipping – worked out. After breakfast, I went upstairs to grab Cardboard Paul and we took him out to take some photos around the casino.

There was a statue of Buck and Winnie in the Harrah's hotel lobby. I called them Kenny and Dolly as they had a close resemblance to the singers. I stood in front of Kenny and Dolly while Pauline took photos of Cardboard Paul and me. A few people started looking at us, which wasn't unusual. A lovely couple came over and said, 'We really have to ask, what is the story with you and the cardboard cut-out? Who is he?' I told them the story about Paul and my promise to him on his death bed. They were sorry for my loss but said that I was brave and they loved the story about Paul and me keeping my promise to him. After our photo shoot, Pauline and I walked next door to the LINQ casino and took Cardboard Paul into the classic car museum there.

We walked into the car museum and I pulled Cardboard Paul out of his bag and carried him around with me in his full size. The owner of the museum came up to me and asked who I had brought with me today. I told him our story and how Paul loved motor vehicles. When I mentioned his love of MINIs, the museum owner told me that they sold one recently and didn't have a MINI in the collection at the moment. He loved our story, wished me well, and hoped we enjoy the collection. I took plenty of photos and videos with Cardboard Paul posing beside the classic vehicles. Paul really loved his cars and did the odd racing and motorkhana in his day. I am sure he would have loved cruising around the car museum.

It was time to head back to our hotel and get ready for our next night of entertainment. We booked tickets to see Human Nature purely because they were an Australian group and we hadn't seen them before. Human Nature was playing next door at the Venetian but it was still a long walk as each casino took up a whole block. We arrived after walking for half an hour and sat really close to the stage. We absolutely loved the night and Human Nature was very entertaining. After the show, we had a chance to meet each of them and they even autographed the CD we bought. Cardboard Paul was not with me but it would have been really cool to get a photo of us with Human Nature.

After the show, we headed back to our hotel's casino for our usual night cap of a Starbucks coffee and a quick play at Keno. We headed back up to our room and packed our bags ready for the next early morning call at 7.30 am for our bags and 9.00 am departure.

In Las Vegas it was very crowded. You could smoke indoors, although there were some limitations around where food was served. Dogs were allowed into casinos and could even stay with their owners in hotels. There were also designated areas indoors for dogs to do their business! Las Vegas had many people shoving things in your face, trying to sell something, wanting you to buy their service, or give you free samples. To walk one block took forever. Although there were buses available, transport was not practical.

Day 8 – Las Vegas to Fresno

*P*auline and I were ready when the porter knocked at the door to collect our luggage. Once our luggage was gone, we checked the room, grabbed our belongings and headed downstairs for our last breakfast at the casino.

Again, we went downstairs and had our same breakfast. We started walking towards our tour bus and found Judy waiting for us and the rest of the group. I shared my concerns about Hurricane Harvey and Judy suggested I contact my travel agent.

3. Las Vegas

The noise level on the bus was high as everyone was sharing stories of what they did the past few days. Most of the group had gone to shows. It was fascinating that we all did something different. Some went to see Cirque du Soleil, David from Wales went to Britany Spears which made us laugh, and considering Britany's target audience wasn't really from his age bracket. Some watched performances from various comedians. We were also interested to hear from our friends from Sydney who loved to shop. We swapped stories of all the clothes, shoes and jewellery we purchased. A few had bought additional luggage to pack their purchases in as they were running out of room in their suitcases. The luggage compartment under the bus was becoming very full. I was wondering how they were going to keep their luggage below the weight limit on the way home. No doubt they would have to pay for extra luggage.

We bid farewell to the neon lights of Las Vegas and made our way towards Fresno. As we headed out onto the highway, our driver became concerned over a red light that was showing on the dashboard. We had driven about half an hour out of Vegas when Piroshka pulled the bus over to the side of the road with a flat rear tyre.

We were stranded on the side of the road in the desert. Conversations started about what food and drink everyone had just in case we were going to be stuck there for a few hours. Between all of us, I think we had enough food to feed an army for a week. Plus, we were stocked up with esky full of water. Piroshka contacted the bus company which then sent out a service person to change the flat tyre. The smokers on the bus were getting anxious and started heading out of the bus and onto the side of the road for a smoke and fresh air. Judy was really concerned and didn't want anyone to leave the bus, so she gave strict instructions for anyone outside to stay close to the bus and not go near the road. At the end of the day, we were all grown adults that were sensible, so Judy had nothing to worry about. It was a hot day and although the bus was cool, it was starting to heat up inside. Lucky for us it only took an hour and a half to get back on the road again. Whilst waiting, we entertained ourselves and I was filming video blogs of my travels.

I also contacted my travel agent via Messenger to let her know of my concerns. We agreed to keep in contact whilst she contacted the hotel. For a while there it wasn't looking good, but I was reassured that everything would be all right. We started planning an alternative if the Houston part of the tour was abandoned. I still had over two weeks before arriving in Houston. As the clean-up was starting, I still had time for the flood waters to subside.

We were on the move again heading across the desert of Nevada and back into California. Our next stop was Barstow where we stopped for lunch and had an opportunity to go shopping at all the outlet malls. I refrained from spending any more money until we hit San Francisco. It was one of our longest days on the road, travelling 636 kilometres to our next destination. We arrived at our hotel and settled in for the night only to pop next door to Denny's for dinner. Again, we unpacked and repacked for the next day's early morning call.

Day 9 – Fresno – Yosemite National Park – Turlock

We were up and ready for our 7.00 am bag collection, early breakfast and 8.00 am bus departure. Breakfast was back to the ordinary, so I just grabbed what I could that looked edible to eat and we were on the road again.

We were headed for Yosemite National Park. It was a bit of a drive and there was the smell of smoke in the air. Bushfires had been raging in the area and the closer we drove to Yosemite the thicker the smoke became. We stopped by a large supermarket to pick up our supplies, snacks and anything else we needed. This place had a pharmacy, clothes, shoes and groceries, it was huge.

Back on the road, the traffic became heavy. As we inched our way towards the park, the scenery was beautiful with huge green trees and streams running alongside the road. We started playing spot the deer. Occasionally, someone would yell out 'deer' or whatever animal they saw and we would all start looking out their side of the window and the cameras clicked away.

3. Las Vegas

After a few hours, we finally arrived at the gates of the park. Judy climbed out to pay the entrance fees and then we were off towards the bus park. Maps and brochures were handed out so we wouldn't get lost. Piling out of the bus, we headed for the main building and sat down to plan our day. Pauline was hesitant to walk the long distance to the different areas, so I decided to take Cardboard Paul for a walk on my own.

Yosemite National Park was amazing and had a beautiful energy about it. We saw many chipmunks which were very similar to squirrels. There were people everywhere from different nationalities. I headed to the waterfall for a look and took some photos. I pulled Cardboard Paul out of his bag and started taking photos of us in front of this huge log with the waterfall in the background. People stared as usual. A couple came over and asked why I had a cardboard cut-out. I told them the story of Paul. They were fascinated and I continued to tell them I was writing a book about our journey and they said they would look out for the book. I also asked them if they were on Facebook and suggested they look up 'Conversations with Paul' where I posted on his escapades. I walked back to where Pauline had been shopping and we grabbed a bite to eat before heading back on the bus.

We all piled back on the bus and Judy did her usual head count. Someone was missing and Judy asked if anyone had seen them. We waited a while but Judy was getting a bit frantic as she didn't want to leave anyone behind. She went to look for them, not letting anyone else help just in case they went missing as well. Finally, Judy found our missing person, young Kieran, who had been waiting for his mum where they said they would meet but mum was already back on the bus trying to phone him. No doubt there was some kind of miscommunication there. We were all back together and off on the road again to Turlock.

We arrived at our next hotel, and as usual, Judy handed out our room keys. Pauline and I found our suitcases and dragged them to the room. Upon opening our room door, we immediately saw one king-size bed. Both Pauline and I looked at each other and started to laugh. I said to Pauline, 'I love you but have only known you for a short time, so, no, I am not sleeping with you.' We went back to Judy to let her know about the mix up – we were not the only ones. It was chaotic with another eight couples having the same issue. Arrangements were made for all those that were single to have their own rooms, so it was the first night since we started on this tour that Pauline and I slept in separate rooms.

Once settled in, we made arrangements to go out for dinner. There wasn't much around except an old western bar next door, so we trekked across car parks and paddocks and through fences to get there. It was definitely a fun walk over there. Once in the bar, it was certainly western, the music was loud, the television blaring, and posters of all different types of sports were on the wooden walls. One of the entrance doors had a big hole in it and was covered up with cardboard. Pauline and I looked at each other and thought, *are we safe?*

Others from the tour were already there ordering beers and the local grub. I ordered beer and cheeseburger while Pauline had a soft drink with hamburger and fries. The food was really delicious although service was slow. I think we were the most customers they had for a while. All the Aussies sat around together, and just chatted and laughed and shared our experiences to date. Overall, we were all having a great time.

After our meal, we went back to our separate rooms and I packed for the next day. I sat up in bed watching television while updating Facebook before nodding off into a deep sleep.

4
San Francisco

Day 10 – Turlock – Sausalito – San Francisco

This morning I had a bit of a sleep in as our bags only needed to be ready by 7.30 am for our 8.30 am departure. I was up and showered before the bags were collected and headed to the breakfast room for something to eat. I met Pauline there and we chatted with the other singles that had trouble with their rooms. The one person that fared really well out of the mix up was Anu who ended up in a huge room with an even larger spa, it was massive.

Our luggage was stored and we were back on the bus heading towards San Francisco. I even started singing *San Francisco (Be Sure to Wear Flowers in Your Hair)*.

Our distance on the road today was much shorter at 166 kilometres, although we couldn't check in to our hotel in San Francisco until 4.00 pm that afternoon. Now we started to see more water from the ocean – the desert was far behind us. It was such a pleasing sight just to see the beautiful colours of the water and the magnificent blue sky with the sun shining.

We arrived in Sausalito for a look around and some lunch. Pauline and I headed across the road from the car park to a little Italian café for a decent cup of coffee as I hadn't had one since arriving in the States. We found a seat out in the front, ordered some coffee and cake and watched the world go by – and yes, people-watch as well. Across the road from the café was the harbour with different types of boats moored.

After our morning tea, we strolled across the road and I pulled out Cardboard Paul from his calico bag and started posing with him against the various sceneries. Again, people walking past would give a side glance and bewildered look, it was priceless. I was starting to enjoy the adventure with Cardboard Paul and felt really comfortable posing with him and telling our story to anyone that asked.

We had plenty of time to explore the quaint Mediterranean style village shops, galleries and breathtaking views. We wandered back to the bus and started chatting with Judy and Piroshka. Judy started to ask me more about Paul and my story. She was really moved and thought I was very courageous doing this tour. We took some photos together with her and Cardboard Paul.

We were back on the road heading towards San Francisco and I was really looking forward to staying there and exploring the city. As we drove closer, you could see the very impressive and expansive Golden Gate Bridge. We drove over the bridge and then headed up into the hills to take in the spectacular views of the bridge and the bay. This place was huge and spread out. I saw this as another photo opportunity, so I dragged Cardboard Paul out again and took plenty of photos.

It was extremely windy where we were and I had to hold on to Cardboard Paul really tight just in case he decided to fly away. We then headed back down nearer to the bridge where we could get a closer look. It was spectacular and the views were even more amazing. I had more opportunities to take photos with Cardboard Paul and then I packed him back into his bag and wandered around the gift shop that had plenty of souvenirs of the bridge and Alcatraz.

Back in the bus, we weaved our way into the heart of San Francisco and headed towards the famous Pier 31. Our visit coincided with the Labour Day holiday weekend, so we were not the only ones who had the same idea to descend on the pier. Not only was manoeuvring through the crowds painful, it just so happened that San Francisco was having the hottest September on record.

We poured off the bus with strict instructions to be back by 3.30 pm to depart for our hotel. Judy provided some brief highlights and places to go and then we were free to explore. The first destination as usual was the ladies' restrooms, but of course we had trouble finding them and when we did there was a long queue. After our toilet break, we started to explore and found a large merry-go-round in the centre of the pier where I took a photo with Cardboard Paul. After a while the crowds were really getting to me and I was feeling very hot and tired.

4. San Francisco

We headed back to our meeting point and found other tour buddies doing the same thing.

Back on the bus we headed to our accommodation for the next few days but had a tour around the Bay City before we checked in. By the time we arrived at our hotel I was ready to just lie on the bed and have a nanna nap. Our room was quaint and had the tiniest bathroom. We unpacked our suitcases, and after taking some room photos with Cardboard Paul, Pauline and I planned on what we wanted to do.

There was complimentary wine between 5.00 and 6.00 pm each night in the lobby so we headed downstairs and found Lynda and Margo. They were heading down to Chinatown and we asked to tag along. We walked for blocks, and considering San Francisco was extremely hilly, it was no mean feat to walk around the streets. We tried to stay at the same level without heading up too many hills. The cable cars went flying past, dinging the bells as they passed. Police and fire engine sirens could be heard loud and clear, and the streets were rather dirty. Although I was really looking forward to San Francisco, my first impressions did not reassure me that I was going to leave this city with fond memories.

After dinner – which wasn't that great – we wandered around Chinatown and all the different shops before heading back to our hotel and our beds for a well-earned rest. Pauline and I hadn't washed any clothes since we arrived so our first plan of attack in the morning was to find a Laundromat. Also, we wanted to hit the closest shopping centre as well to get our nails done.

Day 11 – Free Day in San Francisco

After waking up reasonably early, showering and getting dressed, Pauline and I headed down the hill towards the Westfield shopping centre. As we walked, I had to stop a few times for Pauline to catch up. When we finally arrived at the shopping centre, we found that it only opened at 10.00 am, so we wandered around the area finding a place to have some breakfast. Finally, once we were able to enter the shopping centre, we headed towards Macy's department store.

I was looking for a new wallet as the one I had brought with me was torn and needed to be replaced. In the bag department, we found some bags from Dooney & Bourke, so of course I had to buy one. I found a lovely navy blue bucket bag that was perfect. It was on sale and had further discount – what a bargain! I also found a leather wallet which was what I needed. Pauline also bought a handbag, so we had a really good day shopping. We also found The Cheesecake Factory and put that in the back of our minds to eat later on. We walked further around the shopping centre and found the food court. We grabbed something to eat there before heading back to the hotel.

Walking back to the hotel was no mean feat as it was a straight uphill path. Instead of waiting hours for a cable car, we walked very slowly. We had to stop at every corner for a breather. I was reasonably fit at this time, having lost weight from all the walking, but even this tested me. Back at our rooms we put our purchases on the bed and grabbed our dirty washing and headed out to the Laundromat two blocks across the road. On our way, we found this great little Chinese restaurant and made note to have dinner there that evening. A few loads later and clean washing, we walked back downhill to our hotel. On our way back we found a little place that did manicures and acrylic nails. We made a booking to come back an hour later to have our nails done.

Pauline and I wandered back up the hill into the little nail shop and had our nails done. This shop was tiny and could only fit five chairs – we were practically sitting on top of each other. The ladies were really lovely and chatted with us along with other customers in the shop, asking us where we were from and what we were doing. Pauline and I just wanted manicures and I had a few false nails that had to be removed. I had my nails painted red and Pauline had hers painted with a red tip. Another bargain as it only cost us USD$30.

Later in the evening after drinks in the lobby and catching up with fellow tour buddies, we hiked up to the Chinese restaurant for dinner and it was well worth it. We sat beside a young girl who was studying in university. She explained how she was living with three other people in a small apartment and paying high rent. We were aware that it was very expensive to live in San Francisco.

Day 12 – Alcatraz, City Bay Tour and the Painted Ladies

*T*he Alcatraz prison tour was included in our tour package. We were picked up by Judy and Piroshka to be taken down to Pier 39. We were given our tickets and we lined up to be taken out to the island. On the boat heading towards Alcatraz, I took Cardboard Paul out and we had a couple of photos taken together, other passengers just stared and I smiled. Even Lynda, Margo and Pauline took it in turns to have photos taken with Cardboard Paul.

We arrived at the prison. Due to the steep incline, there was a train that took you up to the top. Pauline and I hopped on the train and was escorted up to the top. While we meandered upwards, the views out to the bay and the Golden Gate Bridge were stunning.

The prison was dark and eerie, I wasn't too keen on walking through the many areas of the prison. We called into the gift shop and found interesting books and souvenirs. We stopped by the theatre area and watched a documentary on the history of Alcatraz. We were always looking for photo opportunities wherever we went, and at Alcatraz I suggested putting Cardboard Paul in a cell. Pauline shot down the idea and insisted that we didn't do that. Once we had explored the prison, we headed back down to the entrance via the train to head back onto the boat.

We had made arrangements with Lynda and Margo to meet up at the boat before heading back to Pier 39 for our City by the Bay cruise. Back on the boat we took in our surroundings as we sailed back into the pier. We bought our tickets and lined up for our cruise. While standing in line, we struck up a conversation with another couple who came from Chicago and the subject of Donald Trump came up. They wanted to distance themselves from him and I commented that the people voted for him. They said, 'Well, we didn't vote for him.'

I said, 'Well, someone did.' They went on to say that not many people voted in the election and I explained that in Australia it was compulsory to vote at our Federal and State elections, otherwise you would be fined. They couldn't believe it and suggested that the USA should adopt the same rules.

Whilst we were queuing up, one of the organisers was being quite rude, telling us all to move along as we were moving towards the boat. In a really sarcastic manner, he said to his colleague, 'It's not rocket science.' We were not impressed!

Once on the boat, we travelled out towards the Golden Gate Bridge and I took some more photos of Cardboard Paul and I. There was also a sighting of whales, although I didn't see them. Lynda did, so at least someone saw it.

From the water, the bay was beautiful and the Golden Gate Bridge looked expansive, big and impressive – an icon.

The four of us arrived back at Pier 39 and together we wandered around the pier and found a place for lunch. After lunch, Pauline and I had a good look around. As I had Cardboard Paul with me, we were taking every photo opportunity available. Pier 39 was famous for the sea lions that congregated in the centre. You could smell and hear the sea lions for miles and we stood there watching them. I made a comment about who was looking at whom, the sea lions were lying around laughing at us humans looking at them, and vice versa.

We met up with Lynda and Margo again later to see the Painted Ladies – made famous on many television shows including *Full House*. We hailed a taxi and piled into it, asking to be taken there. We drove for a while through the streets of San Francisco. When we finally arrived, Lynda, Margo and I – along with Cardboard Paul – stepped out of the taxi, Pauline stayed chatting with the driver.

I took plenty of photos with Cardboard Paul, and the taxi driver asked Pauline what the story was about me and the cardboard cut-out. Pauline told him our story and how we were travelling around the world while keeping my promise to Paul. He asked how long we were together and said that I must have really loved Paul to do what I was doing. He was very touched by our story and he had the kindest eyes. He thought that it was admirable and praised me for doing it. He told Pauline a similar story about losing a loved one. We took the same taxi back to our hotel. Pauline gave the driver a large tip and we wished him well.

Lynda and Margo decided to head back into town to the shopping centre. I said I would join them as I wanted to get some cheesecake from The Cheesecake Factory for desserts that evening. Pauline stayed back in the room and I wandered down the hill with the ladies. While walking towards Westfield where the restaurant was located, there was an elderly lady sitting on the street begging with a cat sitting on her head. I had to do a double-take as I couldn't believe what I was seeing. I had to laugh and when I got back to the room, I told Pauline about the strange sight I had seen. Later that evening – our last night in San Francisco – Pauline and I headed back up to the Chinese restaurant for another delicious meal.

We packed our bags ready for the early morning bag collection at 7.00 am and bus departure at 8.00 am. I packed up all my toiletries and noticed that I had lost a contact lens, which was not smart of me. I had only brought one pair of contact lenses, my prescription glasses and sunglasses. I was not impressed but couldn't do much about it, the lens was gone.

Day 13 – San Francisco to Monterey

We were back on the bus and, again, it was buzzing with everyone sharing their stories and showing what they had bought. I started singing *I Left My Heart in San Francisco* as we drove towards Monterey, though I didn't really feel that way as I was very disappointed that San Francisco didn't live up to my expectations.

We were back on the road, our little tour family all together again, and we realised that our days on this tour were coming to an end. We only had a few more days until we were back in LA.

Today, we only had 180 kilometres to drive through, so we arrived at our destination fairly early and we had a free afternoon to explore. Our first stop was Fisherman's Wharf, known for its historic waterfront. We wandered around the wharf and took some awesome photos with Cardboard Paul, especially the one in front of the Dream Theatre which had the words 'California Dreamin' started in Monterey' across its wall.

After exploring the wharf, we headed over to the Monterey Bay Aquarium for plenty of photo opportunities with Cardboard Paul. It was very interesting how people reacted to him – some would stare, some would do a sideward glance and others would just smile, those game enough would come up and ask why. I loved the aquarium as it was huge and spacious. We could see penguins jumping around and swimming. The aquarium was built as a part of the sea, so it was a natural habitat for all the marine life on display.

After wandering around the aquarium, we had something to eat and then walked down the little street with all the unique shops. Pauline bought a beautiful piece of jewellery in a unique art shop we had wandered into. After our long adventurous day, we were back on the bus heading towards our hotel and looking forward to an early night.

We settled into our room which was one of the better rooms we stayed in throughout the tour. Our usual ritual of unpacking and preparing for what we needed for the night and the next morning was completed, so we wandered down the street to Denny's for dinner. We walked out into the street and Judy asked if she could walk with us. Of course we said yes. Judy started telling us about the issues with another pair of singles on the tour. She was going to ask us to swap with them, but because we were getting on so well, she decided not to ask. I didn't want to get involved in anyone else's business and it wasn't my role to sort it out.

After Judy left us, Pauline and I went into a deep discussion of what we would have done if she had asked for us to swap. We both said a resounding 'no'. It was not our problem but that of the tour director. When we spoke to Lynda and Margo about our conversation, we found out that Judy had actually asked them to swap and they also declined, why should they as they had also made a great connection and formed a lifelong friendship.

After dinner, we walked back to our room still discussing the drama. We packed our bags ready for the next early morning 7.30 am bag collection call. Our days on the road were coming to an end and we only had one more night before heading back to LA.

I find that you will always have one person in a group that is not happy and tend to complain. Unfortunately, in our tour group, we had someone that was not happy about the sleeping arrangements. As we were all on a shared room agreement, the situation escalated throughout the tour and caused much tension and gossip, which was very disappointing. The singles came very close to being separated from their buddies, but we put our foot down. We were very happy with the existing arrangement and didn't want to be separated – plus, we didn't want to be stuck with the problem. To our relief, we stayed as we were and the problematic individual was provided a single room at an additional cost for the last few days of our tour. It certainly put a dampener on the journey, but we were having too much fun to let it disturb or worry us.

Day 14 – Monterey – Carmel – Solvang

We were all back on the bus at 8.30 am for our second to last day on the road as we slowly made our way back to LA. We were on a 27 kilometres drive heading towards Solvang via Carmel, taking in the views of the Pacific Ocean. As we drove into a private road, we had the Pacific Ocean on one side and magnificent houses on the other. We even passed the house that Alfred Hitchcock used in the film *The Birds*. We also saw three whales, plenty of deer, sea otters and seals. We parked along the road next to some gorgeous houses that had spectacular views of the ocean. These houses were very unique, expensive and vast.

We headed towards Carmel-by-the-Sea – a 2.6 square kilometres village nestled in a pine forest. We stopped for a quick toilet break and looked around. The shops were very upmarket and the clothes were expensive. Over the years, there had been many notable people living in Carmel, including Doris Day, Betty White, Robert Louis Stevenson and Clint Eastwood, the former mayor.

Our next stop was lunch in San Luis Obispo where you were not allowed to smoke. The city was also known to have an alleyway with its two walls full of bubble gum stuck to them. All the smokers in the bus were hanging out and waiting for our final destination. Pauline and I wandered around the town and went into a local bar. We ordered two large lemon squashes as it was extremely hot and we were sweating. This also gave us an opportunity to use the restrooms as it wasn't easy finding toilets in these little towns.

After spending a few hours walking around and having lunch, we were on the road again and heading towards Solvang via the old Spanish mission trail. Solvang was known as the town where Denmark was recreated, with picturesque buildings, windmills and flower-lined streets surrounded by the old-world architecture. The odd sighting of the large clogs was intriguing and as soon as we hit the shops that was one of the first places a few of us headed towards to have a look. I am not sure if anyone bought any clogs but I certainly didn't, they were far too expensive.

Once off the bus, I took Cardboard Paul out of his overhead compartment and we headed out taking photos of the two of us in different parts of this lovely town, as well as some photos with other cardboard cut-outs.

Later that night a few of us walked down the road to a recommended Danish restaurant and had a very nice meal. It was our last night on the road together, so a few beverages were consumed.

Day 15 – Solvang – Santa Barbara – Santa Monica – Los Angeles

It was another early start as we had to be on the road at 8.00 am. It was our last day together as a tour family, the mood was very sombre. People we met on the bus were exchanging e-mail addresses and phone numbers, and friending each other on Facebook if they hadn't already. Judy was busy organising bus transfers to the airport as each of us were heading in different directions the next day once we reached LA. Some of us were heading home to Australia and others to New York, Hawaii, England and Wales.

4. San Francisco

From Solvang, it was a short drive south to coastal Santa Barbara where we stopped by the historic mission to take a group photo on the steps. Judy advised us that the company didn't allow her to take group photos of the tour, so we had a couple nominated as the group photographers. Everyone else stood up on the steps in the heat to take a group shot. I had Cardboard Paul standing beside me as we all smiled. Everyone handed over their cameras or mobile phones so they could have a photo to take with them.

People in the group were asking how Cardboard Paul was going and if he was enjoying himself! I said, 'Yes, of course!' He was having so much fun and loved spending time with the group.

After our photos, we headed into the mission to walk around and to find a restroom, which we found at the back of the mission. There was a cardboard cut-out that you could stick your head on, so I put my head on the monk's body and placed Cardboard Paul beside me. I now had another memorable photograph to take away with me.

Our time had come to an end at Santa Barbara and the mission. It was time to head back to the bus and make our way to Santa Monica Pier and the Southern Californian beach with views of the ocean as we drove along the coast. I was really looking forward to seeing Santa Monica Pier since it was featured in many films.

The views as we drove to our next stop were breathtaking and we were all on whale-watch again to see if anyone saw anything from the window's vantage point. All I could see was deep blue water and waves gently breaking on the shoreline. There were many homes jutting out of the cliff with views of the ocean and I wasn't quite sure how they could remain there after years of erosion and sea salt air.

We finally arrived at Santa Monica Pier and scrambled off the bus, heading for the closest restrooms and then a beeline for the pier. The amount of homeless people sitting in the park in front of the pier was surprising and very sad. Judy told us to just be polite and say 'no' when asked for money – but definitely not to give them any money.

There was a bit of a hike to get to the pier, including a steep descent over the freeway. The beach looked beautiful with its clean sand and blue water, although the pier itself was extremely disappointing. It was very crowded with people and amusements. I imagined that it was much larger than what it really was. We wandered around the pier and took plenty of photos with Cardboard Paul, including with other people in the group who wanted a photo with him. He had become part of the group, becoming his own entity. We spoke of him as if he existed, 'don't forget Paul' and 'Paul is very quiet', I would often hear people say as I arrive on the bus.

After exploring the pier, we wandered across the road to the shopping area, finding a place to eat. We found a shopping complex that just happened to have a Cheesecake Factory on the roof. We went inside and was offered a booth and ordered our lunch. The food was really fresh, delicious and inexpensive.

It was time to head back to where the bus was parked. There was a large sign that read 'Santa Monica Pier West End of Route 66', and of course, we had to take a photo with Cardboard Paul in front of that sign.

Piroshka had pulled up with the bus and we boarded the bus for the last time as we headed back to LA. Again, we felt sad that this was it – the end of our tour.

As we drove back into LA, Judy started handing out pieces of paper with times for our transfers to the airport. It had been a long day and the early morning starts were catching up with all of us. We were exhausted and the heat didn't help either.

The bus pulled into our hotel and we piled off, thanking Piroshka and giving her a big hug on our way out, and some of us handing over envelopes of gratuity. Before collecting my luggage, I approached Judy to thank her for the tour and gave her a big hug. I found my luggage and wheeled it in towards the hotel reception desk to check in to our room for the night.

4. San Francisco

As the tour group mingled in the lobby, we said our farewells, hugged and wished each other well and safe travels to wherever they were heading to next. Some of us talked about meeting in the bar later for a farewell drink. Lynda was going to be in New York the same time as me, so we exchanged contact details and arranged to meet up the following Thursday. Margo was also going to be in New York at the same time but wasn't sure if she could catch up due to various tours and arrangements.

Pauline and I headed up to the room, and for the last time, unpacked what we needed for the night before heading downstairs to the restaurant for our last meal together. We didn't have a late night as I had to be up super early in the morning for my 6.30 am transfer to the LA airport. To my surprise, Pauline had snuck down to the gift shop that night and bought me a beautiful pair of silver earrings.

I was up at 5.30 am to head down to the hotel lobby for my transfer. Pauline and I said our goodbyes with a big hug and I was off to New York. I felt sad but also excited that I was on Stage 2 of my journey.

I met Michelle and her son Kieran in the lobby as we were taking the same transfer to the airport. We also happened to be on the same flight to New York before they headed back home to England.

5
New York

Day 1 – Arrival in New York

On the flight to New York, I sat beside this lovely lady, Lara, who was an artist on her way to New York to sell some designs. I had taken some photos of the clouds from the window and she asked me to e-mail her the photos. When I landed, I sent her the photos, although it took some time to send, she did respond saying it was lovely to meet me and that she loved my story about travelling with Cardboard Paul.

I finally landed in New York and went to grab my luggage before heading outside to catch my transfer to the hotel where I was staying for nine days.

It was a fair distance from the airport to Manhattan and the traffic was totally crazy. All I could see was yellow cabs and one-way streets everywhere once we hit Midtown Manhattan. We arrived at the hotel, Club Quarters, located on 40 West and 45th Street. I thanked the driver and paid the fare. I went up to the front desk and was greeted warmly and given my room number and key. I hauled my luggage, went up the lift to the fourth floor and into my tiny room that would be home for the next nine days. As it was early morning, I dumped my luggage in the room, unpacked Cardboard Paul and wandered down to the lobby to grab some maps to explore the city.

The first place to visit was Times Square, which was only two blocks down the road. It was everything I had seen on television, except people were everywhere, and just like Vegas, people were hassling you to get a photo with some kind of character. There were people queuing to get the latest theatre tickets and it was very loud and noisy. There was a heavy police presence and they had some serious weaponry on them, such as semi-automatic machine guns.

After experiencing Times Square, I walked down 5th Avenue to Central Park and there were police everywhere. All you could hear were sirens blaring as fire engines and police cars whizzed past. There were barricades being set up. I found out later that there was a women's marathon being held that afternoon.

It was really warm and I had walked quite a few blocks before I reached Central Park. Again, there were people trying to sell you something on nearly every corner, from horse-drawn carriage rides to Statue of Liberty foam crowns. I saw one woman power walking down the street in a pair of runners – and she was also in her bras and undies, had crazy pink hair and a foam Statue of Liberty on her head! Honestly, you see some sights on your travels!

I finally arrived at Central Park and this place was huge. I was looking for a specific part of the gardens that looked like the painting I had in my family room, but I couldn't find it. I found a bridge with the skyline in the background and pulled Cardboard Paul out and started taking selfies with him. I had a few strange looks, then this lovely lady asked if she could help take the photo of us together. I thanked her and said, 'Yes, that would be great.' I had another person taking our photo which was fun. She didn't really ask about my story or about Cardboard Paul, probably thinking I'm another one of those nutters.

After our photo shoot, I popped Cardboard Paul back in his bag and headed for another section of the park for other photo opportunities. I found some park benches which had lovely little plaques with messages of love nailed to them. I took a few more photos before heading back towards the hotel.

I had been trying to take selfies with Cardboard Paul and there was an art to getting the angle just right. I decided to call into one of the many shops and buy a selfie stick which would make it so much easier to take photos of the two of us. On the way back, I explored around the hotel and found a Starbucks which became my local drinking haunt for the entire time I was in New York.

When I got back to the hotel, I asked the lady at the front desk for a place to have lunch and she suggested a place down the street and around the next corner. I went there and ordered a club sandwich and coffee as I was starving, I hadn't eaten anything since the night before.

By the time I got back to my room I had walked over 10,000 steps – and that was all before lunchtime. I started planning for the next few days and remembered that I was seeing Paul McCartney in concert the next night.

Before I left Australia, I had purchased a 5-day New York Sightseeing Pass and had to collect the book and tickets in Times Square. I decided that I would collect the tickets the next day which just happened to be 11th of September, the 16th anniversary of the September 11 attacks.

After deciding what I wanted to do for the next few days, I went downstairs into the lobby and explored the hotel. It had a large restaurant and a nice lounge area where complimentary soft drinks, coffee and tea were available along with snacks of peanuts, rice crackers and M&M's. I grabbed one of the plastic containers, filled it with M&M's and ventured back into my room.

I had Cardboard Paul propped up standing in the corner just watching over me. If anyone did try and come into my room during the night, they would have got the fright of their lives.

After my very long adventurous day, I hit the pillow and was out straight into a deep sleep.

Day 2 – September 11 in New York

On the anniversary day of the September 11 attacks, New York was very sombre. When I woke up, I turned on the television. It was broadcasting the memorial service live from the World Trade Centre site, reading through all the names that were lost on that fateful day.

I got ready for my big day and night in New York City. I went downstairs to the restaurant for breakfast, and after seeing the prices of the meals, I decided that it would be my last breakfast there.

After breakfast, I headed down to Times Square. After searching and asking many people for directions to the place I needed to collect the 5-day pass, I finally found it. I had to pick them up at Madame Tussauds. The queue just to get in the door was long and I had been queuing for over half an hour before I actually got through the door, in which afterwards I had to queue up again in another line just to pick up the pass.

Whilst I was standing in the queue, I started chatting with a couple standing in front of me. They were from Nelson, New Zealand and asked if I was travelling alone. I told them I was and that I was taking Cardboard Paul around with me, a promise I made to him. They thought it was amazing and really special that I was honouring my promise. They wished me well and that both of us will enjoy the rest of our trip together! I also wished them well on their holiday.

I picked up my tickets and finally headed out the door into the streets. I had also purchased a 3-day pass to jump on and off the big red buses that took you to different sections of Manhattan. I decided that I would do that the next day.

Whilst walking around, I found Grand Central Station and ventured into this amazing building with exquisite architecture. On my walk through the station, I found this marvellous food court downstairs and was able to purchase food to take back to the hotel for dinner. It also sold these moreish macarons which are a favourite and I bought a few for later on.

I was so excited that I was finally going to the Paul McCartney concert in New Jersey. Travelling to New Jersey from Manhattan, New York City was an adventure in itself. I asked Joanna from the front desk what was the best way to get to the Prudential Centre in New Jersey. She suggested the train as the most cost-effective way to travel there, even though I was not familiar with the transport system and would have just taken a taxi.

I walked eleven blocks to the station and when I got there, I asked the man in the ticket booth about purchasing a ticket from Penn Station and he directed me to the ticketing machines. I bought my ticket for USD$6.35 and then asked the same man which platform I had to go

5. New York

to catch the train to New Jersey. Well, he said that it was at a different train station down the street and I should have told him about that before!

Eventually, I found the other Penn train station and went down the stairs into the subway to find out where I could buy a ticket. I finally bought my ticket and asked where I needed to go and proceeded to that platform. The train to New Jersey was similar to the country rail service, so no wonder there was confusion. I was able to get on the train quickly but just needed to confirm with a fellow passenger to ensure I was on the right train. I sat in a carriage and the ticket collector came by to collect tickets. Someone had decided to listen out loud to something from their mobile phone and a man in the carriage started to mumble and asked the person with the phone to be quiet. We were sitting in a quiet carriage where there had to be silence! I felt as if I was sitting in a library and wasn't able to breath too loudly.

I was feeling really nervous and anxious going to this concert in New Jersey once I knew how far it was from where I was staying. I thought of booking a hotel in the area just for the night, but it was extremely expensive – I had already paid more than enough money for the Paul McCartney tickets. I reached my destination and walked out of the station onto the area where I needed to be. Prior to setting off, I checked Google Maps to make sure I knew where I was going. I started to follow a group of people and asked them if they were going to the concert and they said 'yes' but were just waiting for someone, so they pointed me in the right direction. I walked a few blocks and found the venue fairly easily as there were others heading in the same direction.

Once I reached the stadium, I looked around for the closest hotel to ensure that I had a pickup point as I had decided that I was going to take an Uber back to the hotel which I felt was safer than taking the train.

There were plenty of merchandise being sold at the front of the concert venue, I decided to buy a Paul McCartney T-shirt. I spent over USD$40 and was extremely happy. I took some photos in front of the very large billboard advertising the concert.

Security was very tight and there were thousands of people queuing to get in. I was able to find a shorter queue and walked up to security. As I had a half-filled bottle of water in my hand, I had to throw it in the bin as they wouldn't let any drinks in. Once inside I was able to buy a bottle of water but at an exorbitant cost, of course. As it was so hot, I went into the ladies' restroom and changed into my new Paul McCartney T-shirt – now I was dressed for the night.

Paul McCartney's concert was awesome and the best concert I have ever seen. He was on stage for over two hours and played over thirty-five songs from the Beatles, Wings, as well as his new songs. When they played *Live and Let Die*, there was a huge explosion and great pyrotechnics.

Sitting beside me was a lovely father and daughter duo from New Jersey that I chatted with. I told them my story about Paul and they thought it was remarkable and rather brave that I was travelling around the world with a cardboard cut-out.

By the time I left, it was around 11.45 pm, so I walked very fast to the hotel that I spotted earlier. My phone battery was running low and I didn't have any phone coverage as the mobile data service was a hit and miss. So, I looked for Wi-Fi on my phone and managed to connect to free Wi-Fi in front of the hotel. I was able to book an Uber and then waited for another forty-five minutes to be picked up. I felt rather safe as I was in front of the hotel with plenty of other people and police everywhere.

The Uber car finally arrived and there was another person in the back seat. I climbed in, said hello and then started having a great conversation with Jack, the other passenger, whose passions were cars and golf. He was from Hoboken, New Jersey, and after everything I said, he would say 'I hear ya' in that American drawl.

We dropped Jack off and then headed back into Manhattan. We arrived at the hotel and I stepped out and thanked the driver. I went to the front door and found it locked, so I had to swipe my card at the after-hours entrance door and I was back in the safety of the hotel.

I went up to my room, got into my pyjamas and fell into bed. I was exhausted but also extremely happy. I fell asleep with a smile on my face and Cardboard Paul watching over me from his corner spot.

Day 3 – Exploring the Streets of New York

With map in hand and Cardboard Paul in his calico bag, I hit the streets to explore New York. I had to pinch myself knowing that there I was on the other side of the world in one of the most famous cities and there I was walking those streets that were so familiar, like 5th and 6th Avenue and Broadway. My hotel was just around the corner from all these attractions, so walking was the only way to go.

I jumped on the big red New York bus and decided to ride around for the day to have a good look of where the sites I wanted to visit were. I loved seeing the different architectures, especially Art Deco. It had been a long day and I was exhausted.

Day 4 – Empire State Building

On Day 4 in New York, I decided to go to the Empire State Building and took Cardboard Paul with me. Security was fairly tight in these areas and we had to go through scanners as you would do at the airport. I put Cardboard Paul and my handbag through the scanner. When I walked through the scanner, the lady pulled me aside and asked what was in the calico bag. I said it was a cardboard cut-out of my late husband. She called over another security guard in a suit and told him the story. He said I couldn't take Cardboard Paul up to the top with me. I was not sure why because he wasn't a security risk. The security guard couldn't give me a defined answer, so I just told them I understood. No doubt Cardboard Paul was a huge security risk and to say I was disappointed was an understatement.

I went up to the top of the Empire State Building, had a look around, and took some photos and videos. The Art Deco was spectacular in this building. When I came down, I had to go back through security to pick up Cardboard Paul again. They ushered me through and I collected him. The security guard that stopped me in the first place wanted to know the story behind the cardboard cut-out, so I told him briefly about my promise to Paul. He asked if I was travelling alone, how long I was in the USA, where I was from and where I was going to next. He also asked how long Paul and I had been married. After I told him my next journey, how I had already written the book *Conversations with Paul* and how I was writing another book about my adventures travelling with Cardboard Paul. He said that it was good that I was occupied to help me get over my loss! I disagreed and told him that this was not what the trip was about. Paul and I grieved together when he was alive and dying.

I was angry and pissed when I left the building. It made me think again about how people judge you and pigeonhole you just because you have lost a loved one. They just assume that you are grieving. We all grieve differently and at different stages, but this does not give anyone the right to make assumptions that we are doing something to get over our loss or move on. I know you never get over the loss of someone you really love, but life changes, we change, and I changed and recreated my life without Paul, I have no other option.

This trip provided me with a greater understanding of who I was as a person, my purpose, and my 'why I do what I do and what I want to do'.

After the Empire State Building debacle, Cardboard Paul and I headed to the Top of the Rock Observation Deck at the Rockefeller Centre where he was welcomed with open arms and no issues. We even had our photos taken together officially with the tourist photographers that were at all these tourist spots. I took him up to the Top of the Rock and we posed in front of the Empire State Building for photos. I am sure Paul was smirking as I was.

After the Top of the Rock, I wandered down into the NBC shop and bought some T-shirts for my children. I then walked down towards Central Park and ended up in Battery Park where people were gathering to have lunch and lie on the grass to get some sun. I took Cardboard Paul out and sat beside the fountain whilst taking more photos with him. People stared or glanced and had a smirk on their faces but didn't say anything. I then packed Cardboard Paul back in his bag and wandered over to Grand Central Station again to get a feed.

When I was about to cross the road, I fossicked in the calico bag for my glasses. There were no glasses case or glasses to be found. I started to panic as I had already lost my contact lenses. I backtracked where I had been that day, which was some distance. I couldn't find them anywhere. The only glasses I had now to see with were my prescription sunglasses. It looked rather weird in the evening going out with sunglasses on, but I had no other choice. I had another six weeks to go on this *#tripofalifetime*.

Day 5 – Exploring New York's Optometrist

I spent most of the morning searching for optometrists in the area on Google and contacting my son Matthew for my contact lens prescription. I managed to find a few optometrists in the area to buy some new lenses. I thought if I could get contact lenses, I would be able to get by for the rest of my travels.

I walked down a block near Times Square and found a place, La Bleau, that sold prescription eyewear. I walked in and was greeted by this beautiful lady named Izabella who was more than accommodating. Izabella gave me some lenses to try and I was fortunate that my magnification was available. She also suggested that I buy new prescription glasses as I had another four weeks of travelling before heading home. I agreed that it was a great idea and we picked the perfect pair. All I had to do was get my prescription.

I contacted my optometrist at home for my prescription, the script was e-mailed to me, and within 48 hours, I had a new pair of glasses and a 3-month supply of contact lenses. Izabella went over and above to help me with my dilemma. I was extremely grateful.

The message for me with all this drama of losing things was that no matter what was thrown at me, there was no use worrying or stressing as there will always be a solution no matter where I was in the world.

After sorting out my contact lenses, I was off touring again. Another big day walking and I fell into bed to the sounds of New York outside my window – until I was woken up at 3.00 am to the sounds of drilling outside my window. I was not impressed. I even recorded the noise in case people didn't believe me.

Day 6 – Night Cruise of New York

On Thursday night, Lynda – from our California tour – and I took Cardboard Paul down to the bay and we toured around New York on the night cruise. We went past the Statue of Liberty and viewed all the gorgeous buildings at night. The skyline was spectacular, especially as the sun was setting and the lights in all the buildings came on. The night was really mild and warm and the skyline stunning. We had plenty of photo opportunities with Cardboard Paul and Lynda was happy to catch up with him again.

We then went to B.B. King's Blues Club & Grill for a meal and had the fortune of seeing a James Brown impersonator singing with his band. The performance topped off a great evening, plus the food and beer were really good.

New York was very loud, busy and dirty plus some areas really smelled. Rubbish was dumped out on the streets for the garbage collectors to collect very early in the morning. They said it's the city that never sleeps and I could really relate to that. There were massive building projects happening around the city area and the noise was constant throughout the evening and into the early morning.

People were impatient and didn't wait for the little green man to walk. You take your life in your own hands as cars, people, trucks and bikes didn't necessarily pay attention to the traffic signals. The traffic in the city centre was absolutely crazy and insane, one-way streets and traffic jams everywhere you look. Cars would block intersections and didn't pay attention to the police that were manning the intersections.

People seemed to be in a rush and you can tell the difference between the tourists and the locals. The locals tended to keep to the right, while many tourists do the opposite and keep to the left which can be very confusing with many people dodging or running into each other if they were not paying attention.

Many people – like in every other city or town – were looking down at their phones or had headsets in their ears. Look at what they are missing by looking down on their devices! I enjoyed looking up at all the people, the sky and the buildings that surrounded me, it was a wonderful experience.

I felt very safe in New York as there was a very large police presence, especially around Times Square. Each of the attractions had security in which you have to go through like the airport.

Day 7 – World Trade Centre Site and 9/11 Memorial & Museum

Whilst everyone was sleeping, I was being adventurous and caught the subway to the World Trade Centre site and the 9/11 Memorial & Museum. I didn't take Cardboard Paul with me, as it was not necessarily appropriate, plus carrying him around in the heat became very tiring.

As soon as I stepped out of the subway into the area, I got the tingles – big time. It just brought back so many memories of that day, a day I will never forget along with the rest of the world. The museum was amazing but also very sombre, emotional and confronting. There were plenty of photos, videos and items from that devastating day. There were voices of people who were in the towers and those of the survivors. I couldn't stay in there for long and quickly made my way through the exhibits and back out to the sunshine to see the two reflecting pools covering where the towers actually stood. They were adorned with flowers left during the memorial a few days before. An amazing tribute to all those that lost their lives, as well as to the survivors.

On my way back to the hotel, I stopped off for a Starbucks coffee and famous cinnamon rolls. I was glad I was walking as much as I was, as I was losing weight, not putting it on.

I also stopped by the glasses shop to collect my new glasses, which were fantastic and looked really good on me. I thanked Izabella again and she wished me well on my travels with Cardboard Paul.

Day 8 – Relaxing Day Out in New York

This morning I sat on my good Ray-Ban sunglasses and broke the arm off them, so I needed new ones. I was not sure what was going on, with losing and breaking the gear I used to see with. No doubt there was a message in it for me. I was able to pick up a very nice pair of sunglasses from a street vendor for just USD$10 – I was on a win.

After my purchase, I headed down to Battery Park where I had a relaxing day with Cardboard Paul. We sat in the sunshine watching people go by, which we often did when Paul was alive. I was getting the odd stare but believed that New Yorkers were used to seeing really strange people in the streets.

I ventured down to Rockefeller Centre again to have a really good look around the ground floor and just enjoy the magnificent Art Deco architecture.

On the way back, I headed to Starbucks for a coffee and I pulled Cardboard Paul out for a photo opportunity.

Lynda and I caught up again for dinner at the local Irish pub where we had a light snack and drinks before heading to B.B. King's Blues Club & Grill again to see a cover band playing Motown music. It was such a great night. Lynda and I had so much fun together.

Day 9 – Seeing Paul McCartney in New York

This was my last full day in New York. I strolled around the streets and ended back at Grand Central Station. I bought some food for dinner before I headed off to my second Paul McCartney concert at Madison Square Gardens that evening. I walked down 5th Avenue and took some photos of the display in Saks Fifth Avenue.

I stumbled across St Patrick's Cathedral where I lit two candles, one for Paul and one for Mum. It reminded me of the time Paul and I would visit St Paul's Cathedral in Melbourne when he was going through his treatment at Peter MacCallum Cancer Centre. We would light a candle hoping and praying that he would beat the dreaded cancer that was taking over his body. The candle I lit was to remember him in spirit and know that he was still around me.

It was time to wander back to the hotel to get ready for the Paul McCartney concert and I had to hold in my excitement. I wore my new Paul McCartney T-shirt with pride as I strolled down the streets of New York.

I walked eleven blocks to get to Madison Square Garden, and the closer I got the more people I saw that were heading there. I finally arrived and as I had time to spare, I wandered through this very large Target store which was very interesting, especially the people that were shopping there.

Once at Madison Square Garden, I went through security easily and found my seat. I was really close to the stage and was on the floor next to the sound technicians, they were awesome seats. I sat next to two ladies, they were sisters-in-law. I found out that one of their husbands worked on Wall Street, so no doubt that they had a lot of money. She was flaunting it and being very drunk and obnoxious. She bragged about being in Sydney, Australia for business and living in Singapore and Bangkok, and going to Bali. I tuned out fairly quickly and felt really sorry for the sister-in-law who had to put up with this outlandish behaviour. She also bragged about buying New York Rangers VIP tickets for the season at USD$17,000 in Madison Square Stadium.

The three seats in front of us were empty, bar one old man that continued to stay standing throughout the concert. I didn't pay over US$250 to see the back of this guy. He also spilt beer which landed on the floor right in front of us. A mop was summoned and spilt beer was cleaned up but it made the floor even more slippery than it was, so I had to be very careful when standing up and dancing on the spot.

I took heaps of photos and videos but was sad that I didn't have Cardboard Paul with me. He was tucked home safely in the hotel in the suitcase ready for my flight to Houston. I also wasn't sure if I could get him through security at the stadium. Considering that other people had signs up, why couldn't I have Cardboard Paul standing up there as well?

Again, Paul McCartney's concert was awesome and the best, even greater than his concert in New Jersey. I think the venue really made the difference as Madison Square Garden was smaller and more intimate, plus I had superior seats that were closer to the stage.

After the concert, I headed back the eleven blocks to the hotel. As it was past midnight, I walked extremely fast and accidentally walked one street up too far. It was all right though, as I was between 5th and 6th Avenue, so I started to walk along 5th Avenue. It was an eye-opener to see homeless people sleeping on the streets considering that 5th Avenue was where all the high-end shops and designers were. I was keeping up with a couple that were walking just as fast as I was, then I took over them. It took me around twenty minutes to walk back.

I hit the pillow with Paul McCartney singing in my head.

It was a very early start as I needed to be up at 5.30 am to be ready, packed and down at reception by 6.35 am. I headed down to reception at 6.15 am and the shuttle company picked me up at 6.20 am. Luckily I was already prepared downstairs. When I got on the bus it was fairly full of people. We picked up one lady from a few streets away and just after we left her hotel, she started looking for her phone and couldn't find it. Considering we had to wait for her in the first place and then for her not having her phone, the passengers were getting a little agitated. So, we had to go around the block again to drive pass the hotel so she could pick up the phone that she forgot. The driver apologised to the passengers for the inconvenience, but the culprit did not say one word. Common courtesy would suggest that you would have at least said sorry, but no! Not this one! It didn't really delay my schedule as I had two hours before boarding my flight. So, I relaxed, grabbed something to drink and eat before heading into security.

I also heard that Donald Trump was heading into the United Nations Headquarters in New York that day and there were traffic gridlocked and bridges and roads blocked off for him. We didn't have any delays, although the bus driver was crazy and didn't listen to any of the sirens of the emergency vehicles with lights flashing behind her, she did not budge! I was so thankful that I left New York when I did as Hurricane Jose was heading up into that area and was predicted to cause some rough weather for the next few days.

6
Texas

Day 1 – New York to Houston

The flight from New York to Houston was interesting as the security were being difficult and expected you to jump through hurdles for them. I can understand that they needed to go through the processes, but at the end of the day, we are all humans and a little courtesy could go a long way.

I took my shoes off to go through the scanner, then they waved me back saying I was all right because I had pre-clearance to go through. I was glad that I had Cardboard Paul tucked in my suitcase, as taking him through some of these security checks would have been a huge headache.

When I arrived at the gate, the service attendant wouldn't let me board the plane with three bags. I had my wheelie bag, computer bag and handbag, so I had to make it into two bags. I pulled my laptop out of its bag and shoved it into my handbag, and then quickly rearranged my wheelie case and shoved the computer bag into that. I was surprised it fit, and if it didn't, I was going to pull everything out of it and dump them on the spot. Fortunately, it all turned out well in the end.

On the plane, I sat next to a fellow author, Glen Eldridge, who wrote *We Are Woodstock*. He told me he was sixty-seven years old but he didn't look anything like it and looked great for his age! He also told me that he had an ex-wife, a daughter and a grandchild, with another on the way. I chatted with him about the hurricane in Houston.

We also talked about music including Paul McCartney, Beatles and all the old rock and roll – the good – music. He was telling me about Houston, San Antonio and Austin. He highly recommended Austin, so it was a shame I had only planned to be there for one day! I had to wait and see how it went. If it was awesome, I could always come back and spend more time there.

I told him about Paul, as well as the time in Vegas where Judy suggested taking Cardboard Paul to the Vegas show. He thought it was very funny and we laughed. I also showed him some photos of Cardboard Paul and he said Cardboard Paul really looked lifelike and thought it was a great story.

The flight attendants were hilarious and humorous when chatting to passengers and especially during the pre-flight safety demonstration. An Asian lady sitting opposite from us coughed, spluttered and left dirty tissues in the pocket behind the seat and then put a mask on over her mouth, it was disgusting. We also had a priest sitting behind our seats, so I think we were safe! If anything did go wrong, we would at least have someone that would pray for us!

My first stop of Houston, Texas was a two night's stay, and then I would be headed to San Antonio by Greyhound bus.

I was hoping that there was not too much damage in Houston after Hurricane Harvey, which hit two weeks before I was scheduled to arrive. I had been in constant contact with Alyssa, my travel agent, regarding the clean-up and if my accommodation would still be available. By the time I arrived in Houston, majority of the flooding had subsided – you would never have thought there had been a hurricane in town.

My accommodation at Houston was the DoubleTree by Hilton, which was really good. The staff were friendly and it was located two blocks away from a very large and opulent shopping centre.

I arrived and the reception gave me my room number and key and I went upstairs to unpack Cardboard Paul. I then wandered down to reception again to find the nearest post office and if there were washing machines available in the hotel as I hadn't washed any clothes since San Francisco.

I wandered over to the shopping centre, and as I went outside, the heat and humidity hit me in the face. By the time I reached the shopping centre, I was drenched in sweat. This shopping centre was huge, with very large high-end department stores and even an ice-skating rink on the ground floor. It was a shopaholic's dream come true.

I finally found the post office and purchased a box. I was carrying excess weight and didn't want to keep touring with it, so I decided to send items that I wasn't using back home via mail. After exploring the shopping centre, I headed back to the hotel and up to the laundry room to do a few loads of washing. I was getting hungry and wanted to eat, so I decided to stay in and eat at the hotel bar. I am so glad I did.

I sat at the bar next to a gorgeous young lady and ordered a Merlot and chicken tenders with fries, which were very nice. I started chatting with three other people at the bar, Craig, Henry and Madeline. They were from nearby of Austin and they advised me that Austin was a really great place to stay, pity I was only going to be there overnight and wouldn't have a chance to look around. We had a great night and awesome conversation. Henry showed us some old photos and told the story of how he had been in the Navy when he was younger and had travelled around the world including Perth, Australia. He also knew one of the American golfers that died in the plane crash that hit Essendon DFO shopping centre. It was certainly a small world. I connected with Henry on LinkedIn and Madeline on Facebook.

After letting the group know my story of travelling with Cardboard Paul, Craig and Madeline started following *Conversations with Paul* on Facebook. Craig paid for my dinner and wine and I was extremely grateful. I let him know that he didn't have to, but Craig said, 'You are such a brave lady travelling by yourself and I admire you.'

It was getting late and we said our farewells and headed off to our own rooms.

The best part about my travels was meeting and chatting with new people and sharing our stories and creating memories. I am forever grateful for being able to share my stories as well as hearing all the different stories and accents.

Day 2 – NASA Space Centre

I had asked my travel agent to book a tour for me to NASA as I had always been fascinated with outer space and the sky. I even wanted to be an astrologer when I was younger.

The NASA Space Centre was located on the other side of Houston, so I caught a taxi from the front of the hotel. I had a very lovely driver. He was asking about my travels and I told him the story of Cardboard Paul. He dropped me off where I was supposed to be and I said farewell. He gave me his card and said, 'Call me if you need a lift.'

I waited in front of the Marriott where I was supposed to meet my tour group. There were three others on the tour to NASA, David from Belfast and a couple from New Zealand. We started off on our tour and within ten minutes of taking off, the bus broke down. We had to wait for another bus.

Once the other bus arrived, we did a quick tour around Houston and was amazed by how huge the place was and that all the restaurants and cafés were built underground due to the heat. The place was beautiful and I was disappointed that I was only there for two days. It was a city I would put on my list to revisit if I was touring the USA again.

After our Houston city tour, we headed onto NASA. I didn't take Cardboard Paul with me on this tour but I wish I had because there were cardboard astronauts everywhere. I hung out with them and took heaps of photos.

We went on the big tour around NASA and visited the old control room for the Apollo missions. It was like stepping back into the 60's as it was still in the same condition as it was back in the era. After mission control, we headed out to where the big planes were that escorted the space rockets back. We also went to where they conducted tests on the space suits, rockets and any other space equipment.

This place was fascinating and I loved every minute of it. It was well worth the time to explore this amazing place. Many people would mistakenly say, 'Houston, we have a problem', but the actual statement

6. Texas

by James A. Lovell Jr. was 'Uh, Houston, we've had a problem'. The other famous saying is 'The *Eagle* has landed', whereas the full statement was 'Houston, Tranquillity Base here. The *Eagle* has landed', by Neil Armstrong.

After our tour, we arrived back at the Marriott and I had to get back to my hotel on the other side of town. An Uber was organised from the front of the Marriott by one of the ushers.

The Uber driver took me back to my hotel and I felt totally ripped off as I was charged USD$40 excluding tips, while the taxi driver that dropped me off from Hilton only charged me USD$23. The Uber driver was constantly on the phone and snorted and sniffed all the way back, he was totally disgusting.

That night I sat at the bar again and Henry was there having a quiet drink, we had a quick chat and then he had to go. I bid him farewell and he wished me well on my tour around the world.

On my last day in Houston, there was a very handsome stranger standing next to me as we rode down the elevator. I complimented him on his suit and said that I liked a man in a good suit. He was concerned that the suit was wrinkled, but I disagreed and told him it looked really good.

When do we actually take the time to tell people that they look fantastic? Are we too quick to judge and look at the negatives? I certainly made that man's day by giving him a compliment.

I arranged for the taxi driver that dropped me off at the Marriott downtown the previous day to take me from my hotel to the bus station. I paid him USD$40 but it was worth it, he was a lovely man and he told me I was a very strong woman, travelling around the world by myself.

Day 3 – Houston to San Antonio

It was time to say goodbye to Houston as I travelled by Greyhound bus to San Antonio. As we were travelling to the bus station, there was a group of homeless people camped under a bridge. It was extremely sad to see the amount of homeless people throughout the USA.

I thanked the taxi driver and dragged my luggage into the bus station and waited with all the others for the next bus out of Houston. The bus station was a real eye-opener and I felt really out of place and questioned whether it really was the right decision to take the bus and train through Texas. Fortunately, it was definitely an experience and I was able to see some countryside. It was very hot and humid and my glasses fogged up as I walked outside – it was like a sauna. Our bus was ready to be boarded but was in desperate need of repair with the overhead shaking and looked as though it would fall down every time we went over a bump.

Halfway through our journey, we had a stop for fifteen minutes to go to the toilet and grab something to eat. The bus driver came back on the bus and asked all the passengers if there was anyone missing. I turned around and started laughing at the passenger diagonally opposite me. He asked me which part of Australia I came from as he picked up on the accent. I told him Melbourne and he told me that he came from St Kilda. He looked like a surfie type. We exchanged a few pleasantries and then continued with what we were doing. I listened to music and stared out the window. We didn't really chat after that.

We finally arrived safely at San Antonio and it was nowhere as vast as Houston. I looked for a taxi and headed towards my hotel for the next two nights, Holiday Inn Downtown Market Square. The hotel wasn't close to any amenities, which made me feel isolated. The accommodation was appalling and the reception staff was no better. When I arrived at my room, the door was ajar and I had to lug my two suitcases with no assistance. I finally entered my room and had to use my foot and arm to slam the door shut as it wouldn't close properly. I took my shoes off and noticed that the carpet was wet and I started to wheeze. I also went to switch on the television and that didn't work either.

I was beyond caring, so I contacted the hotel reception and told them about my issues. They advised me that they would contact the engineer for further information and direction. Within the hour I received a call from reception telling me that they were changing my room. I had a knock on the door and the bell boy gave me the key to my new room which was only two doors away. I gathered all my belongings and moved rooms. I didn't even shut my door as it was too difficult to shut in the first place.

Whilst I was moving rooms, the room next door to mine had the handyman trying to fix the door because it wasn't working at all. I sympathised with the gentleman who was waiting patiently for the door to be fixed. I finally settled down in my new room and wandered downstairs to the bar and restaurant for a meal and drink.

I was thankful that I was only staying here for two nights.

Day 4 – San Antonio

The next morning as I was heading out the door for the next part of my journey of exploring San Antonio, I walked past a guy that was standing outside his room last night and I said, 'Hello, how are you going?' He then went on to tell me that his room was full of mould and they had to move. I just shook my head and was glad I was out of there the next day.

As I was far away from the city, I grabbed an Uber and went into town with Cardboard Paul to the Alamo, which was very interesting and had beautiful gardens. I walked around the area and was deeply moved by its sad history of bloodshed. There were people dressed up in period costumes, taking the tourists back in time. I wandered around the beautiful gardens and pulled Cardboard Paul out and took numerous photos. Not too many people looked at us and went on with their business, which was a change.

Many photos later, I headed out and walked towards the shopping centre. I found a food court where there were different types of cuisines available. I then proceeded to Macy's Department Store to see what they had. I ended up buying two new handbags as my Blue Illusion handbag started to fall apart. I also bought a new pair of headphones as I was getting ear infections from the current ear plugs I was using.

I walked along the picturesque river and took Cardboard Paul out for photos. It was very hot and humid, so I headed back to the hotel. I sat beside the pool and wrote some reflections on my journey to date. It was just nice to sit beside the pool and swim. When I got too hot, I jumped into the cold-water spa, which was very relaxing.

Day 5 – San Antonio to Austin

I was back on the road again and this time I was travelling by train from San Antonio to Austin. It was a really early start, I had to be at the train station before 6.45 am as the train was leaving at 7.00 am. I booked a taxi to take me to the station at 6.00 am and arrived well before the departure time. Again, the station was very interesting with all types of people. The train wasn't that comfortable as the seats kept rocking back and forth. As it was really early in the morning, I nodded off for a few minutes and then just sat back, relaxed and listened to my music. The journey took two hours and the breakfast cart was open, but the choices were not that promising, I didn't even attempt to get anything.

I arrived at the Austin station and had to wait a while whilst the taxis turned up to collect passengers. For a moment, I was getting worried as I had no Wi-Fi or phone coverage. After waiting about half an hour, with most of the passengers gone, a taxi arrived taking me to my next accommodation, Crowne Plaza. I arrived at the hotel and was looking for something to eat as it was still relatively early in the morning. I wandered into the hotel restaurant and a lovely waitress called Sandra was able to assist me with some brunch, which I was extremely grateful for as I hadn't eaten for a few hours.

Whilst eating my meal, a couple were organising their wedding and considered the hotel for their reception. The couple were really over the top and wanted so much. The bride reminded me of a bridezilla.

As I was only in Austin overnight, I didn't have the energy to explore around the city and decided to stay around the hotel and catch up on some well-earned rest.

Day 6 – Austin to Waco

As I was travelling to Waco via bus again, I was able to organise a courtesy bus at the hotel reception. The driver, Rudy, was very nice and helped me carry my bags into the terminal.

The bus terminus was the same as all the others in Texas, filled with a different mix of people and they were very interesting to watch. I boarded my bus and we were headed to Waco which was a few hours away. Country and Western music played in the background courtesy of the driver and I was tapping the old foot to the beat. I think I really looked out of place but it was an experience and at least this bus was in much better condition than the last one I took.

I arrived in Waco and hailed a cab with an Uber driver. He decided to rip my head off with the fare as there was a big football game straight across the road from where I was staying. The taxis were in demand so they could ask for whatever payment they wanted.

I arrived at my accommodation, the Red Roof Inn, and it was terrible. I went up to reception and the guy behind the counter was certainly a sandwich short of a picnic as he had no idea what I was saying. It must have been my accent. I was shown my room and when I walked in, I nearly started to cry. I was totally disappointed with all this shocking accommodation throughout Texas and I started looking for alternatives. I contacted my travel agent who asked me to sit tight for the time being whilst she organised an alternative accommodation.

I was starving as I hadn't eaten all day, so I went down to reception again to ask where the nearest café or restaurant was for a feed. Again, he couldn't understand my accent but pointed me in some direction and I walked over. I had been walking for a while and it was extremely hot and humid, plus I was sweating. I walked over the Waco River via the bridge and found some shops that looked reasonable.

I went into Cricket's Grill and Drafthouse and was greeted warmly and shown my seat. The attendants were very friendly and loved my accent. The girl serving me was lovely and brought out a selection of beers for me to try. I tried all of them but nothing caught my fancy. She brought out a few more and I found one that wasn't too bad, so I ordered a large jug of that. It was thirsty work walking from the hotel to the restaurant. I ordered chicken tenders with fries, it was a huge but delicious serving. I was watching the college football game on the television screen and was really interested and got hooked. I paid my bill and walked back to the hotel.

My travel agent was able to organise better accommodation and I moved out. I called an Uber and then went to the hotel reception to return the key. He looked at me blankly and I just walked out of the door not looking back, shaking my head all the same.

My Uber driver wasn't that much better as she drove into the driveway, went right past me and then out the other end. She then did a U-turn, came back, almost driving right past me again until I hailed her down. She gave me this dumb look and said something to the effect of, 'Oh, I didn't see you.' I am not sure what I had walked into but I was getting a bit nervous. Fortunately, we arrived at my new accommodation at the Quality Inn & Suites and I was very happy as this was more upmarket and to my standard.

I finally arrived into my new room and started to unpack. I realised that I had lost my selfie stick, which I had probably left at the Red Roof Inn – no way was I going back there. I finally relaxed, unpacked Cardboard Paul and took some photos of him lounging around the room. I was really looking forward to the next day and going to Magnolia Market, with hopes of catching a glimpse of Joanna and Chip Gaines.

I learnt a good lesson for the day when ordering coffee. Starbucks was everywhere and there was really no other choice for coffee. I went through the menu trying different coffees out and I thought the Americano would be good, not knowing that it was black coffee. Luckily, I only ordered a small size and it perfectly balanced out the cinnamon coffee cake I had.

Day 7 – Waco

I was ready to explore Waco. The first port of call was down near the river and along the banks where they had huge sculptures of cattle and drovers. I pulled Cardboard Paul out and started taking photos. I turned around and there was a blue MINI across the road. I knew Paul was with me.

After my photo session along the river, I walked into town towards Magnolia Market. When I arrived, it was closed. I went up to the door to read the opening times, and of course, it wasn't open on Sundays. I was extremely disappointed as this was my only reason to visit Waco. As I was headed out to Dallas the next morning by bus, I wasn't going to drag my suitcases over there and back to the station in the heat.

I took some photos of Cardboard Paul and packed him away. I was making my way back to the hotel when a car pulled up beside me. A few gentlemen leaned out the window to ask me if Magnolia Market was opened. As soon as I opened my mouth and spoke, they asked where I was from. I told them I was from Melbourne, Australia and I was travelling with Cardboard Paul. They couldn't believe it and told me I was very brave and that it was an honour to meet me.

Day 8 – Waco to Dallas

I was up early and was able to get a courtesy lift from the hotel to the bus station. The driver was a lovely lady and I tipped her when I arrived at the station. I checked in at the station and the attendant asked, 'Have you got one to go under?' referring to my suitcase, and I said, 'Yes, it came from down under.' I always take the opportunity to be positive and make someone laugh or smile and that morning I accomplished that.

I then sat waiting for the bus to arrive. There was a lady mopping the floor, swearing under her breathe and barking at customers if they walked anywhere on her freshly mopped floor. Again, the bus station was an eye-opener as there was a lady sitting there half-dressed, complaining about money and not having enough – I don't think she was the full quid! She walked in and out to have a cigarette and then back in again, mumbling to herself. Someone sat beside her – who was also dubious – and she continued to complain until they had enough and walked off.

The Greyhound bus arrived and I was back on the road, which wasn't too bad as the bus went through the highway. I sat back relaxed, put my headphones on and listened to music as I stared out the window watching Texas go by, making my way to Dallas.

I arrived at the Dallas bus station and asked the attendant where I could catch a taxi. He gave me directions and I headed out the door to find a ride to my next hotel. There was a taxi out front but the taxi drivers were too busy talking and totally ignored me until they realised that I actually needed a ride. The fare to the hotel was a complete rip off again as they charged me USD$40 from the bus station to the hotel, which wasn't that far out of town.

I walked into my accommodation and it was simply appalling. I stood at the counter and was so upset that I had to hold back the tears. I grabbed my key to the room and asked if someone could assist me to get my bags up the stairs to where my room was located. After waiting for ten minutes, I thought, *stuff this*. I was so angry and upset I just dragged my luggage up the stairs to the first floor. By the time I reached the top, the man arrived to assist and I said, 'Don't worry about it.' When I got into the room, I burst into tears. This place was out in the sticks and nowhere near anything other than a Denny's next door. The room was mediocre. I contacted my travel agent again who then tried to arrange for a different accommodation, but it was further out, so I told her not to worry about it as I was only here for two nights.

After my meltdown, I had a good talking to myself and organised a taxi for the next day to go into town and explore Dallas and the history of John F. Kennedy.

Day 9 – Dallas

In the morning, I went next door to Denny's for breakfast, which was really good. I jumped into the taxi that I ordered the day before and headed into Dallas. The taxi driver dropped me off near where all the tourists were. I thanked him and paid him the fare plus tips, which was cheaper than the drive from the bus station to the hotel. I proceeded to explore the area.

Feeling so much better than I did the day before, I ventured into Dallas and sought to learn more about John F. Kennedy (JFK) and his assassination. It was a whole tourist industry surrounding that fateful day back in 1963. I was directly opposite to where JFK's car came down and he was shot from the window of the book depository store. The store was now an entire museum dedicated to him and that day. You could even go into the same room where that fateful shot was fired.

I booked in for the one hour tour around Dallas that followed the events of that day in November 1963. I climbed onto the trolley car and was greeted by Robert, the driver, who was very friendly. As soon as I spoke, he said, 'You're from Australia.'

'Bingo,' I said. We waited for a few moments and another two gentlemen from Chicago, Michael and Chris, joined us. We started chatting amongst ourselves with the driver and they were trying to work out my nationality – I wasn't giving the game up. They were guessing England, Irish, Swedish and even Massachusetts. Robert was playing along as well. In the end I confessed I was Australian, and they said, 'Oh no, I love your accent.' I told them the story about how I was travelling the world by myself with Cardboard Paul and they couldn't believe me. I told them I was writing a book and they said to make sure I mentioned them and say that they were very tall and handsome – the good-looking ones! I laughed and agreed to include them in the book and say they were very nice guys, very funny and also very cute – but I couldn't say they were very tall, just saying!

Our tour began where JFK and Jackie Kennedy started in the parade through Dallas and we listened to the history of how it came about that they were driving in an open topped car through the streets, which wasn't the norm. The tour took us through all the streets where the car went, where JFK was shot, past the hospital and also where Lee Harvey Oswald ran and hid. This tour was fascinating and I really enjoyed it.

After we returned, I jumped off the trolley and said farewell to all the guys and headed up to the book depository store where there was a display on the history of JFK and his assassination. I was given headphones and a playing device so I could listen to the story. This place was massive and impressive and I even stood at the window where the fatal shot was taken. It was very eerie and surreal. After the self-guided tour, I went back into the gift shop and purchased some items for my daughter Sarah who was a big fan of JFK. She wrote a history project for high school a few years ago on JFK. I also purchased a book for Mum.

After spending more money than intended, I ventured across the road to have a look at the coffee shop for something to eat. I then walked further around town, past this gorgeous little church and lovely gardens. It was time to head back to the hotel. Whilst on my travels, I saw heaps of MINIs and my taxi driver's name was Paul. Paul was travelling with me that's for sure.

I arrived back at the hotel and headed off to Denny's for dinner and then back to my room to pack for the next day as I was flying out to Paris. I was so looking forward to seeing the place on the top of my list of cities to visit, and was also glad to see the back of Texas as it had been a disaster, except for a few highlights.

I was up early, showered and dressed very quickly, and walked out of that horrible room. I headed down to the hotel reception to wait for my taxi to take me to the airport. I arrived at Fort Worth Airport to catch the plane to Paris and was so looking forward to the next stage of my journey. As I was early for my flight, I had to hang around the airport and I decided to get a bite to eat before the long haul journey. Going through security was easy and I had no issues.

I was very happy to say farewell to the USA. I boarded my flight for Paris and didn't look back.

7
Paris

Day 1 – Arrival in Paris

I finally arrived in the city I always wanted to visit – Paris, the city of love. Unfortunately, here I was by myself with no one to share the experience with since losing the love of my life in May 2016. Paul and I talked about travelling to Paris for years but never got around to doing so. Even as he was having his last PET scan two weeks before he died, Paul was telling all the nurses that as soon as he was well, we would travel together, especially to Paris and London. At least he was still with me, in spirit and in cardboard.

After landing in Paris, it felt very strange seeing everything written in French. I was feeling very tired and emotional as I came out to the open area. I couldn't find my transfer to the hotel, so I went up to the information counter and asked in a mix of broken French and English where I needed to be to connect with my transportation. I gave the lady behind the counter the piece of paper I had with the transfer details on it. She called the contact number and then gave me the details of where I had to go to meet my ride.

I walked out the doors again looking for the vehicle and waited for about fifteen minutes with no luck. I walked back to the information counter and a different lady was there. Again, I asked where I needed to go to meet this transfer and she gave me the same instructions. By this time, I was getting very frustrated and anxious.

I went out the same door again but decided to walk in the opposite direction. I found a person standing, having a cigarette outside a totally different door, holding a sign with my name on it. I was so relieved. I gave the man my bags and he placed them in the back of the van. I climbed into the front seat. And saw that the van was already full of other travellers, most of which were Australians. I sat beside an elderly gentleman from central New South Wales; we started chatting about our holidays and what we had planned during our stay in Paris.

It was funny as I was the last one on – and probably held up the group for a while – but I was the first one off. I arrived at my accommodation for the next five days, Hôtel Royal Garden Champs-Elysées. The weather was beautiful, sunny and warm. I was happy, relieved and excited. The next stage of my journey was beginning.

After only being in the country for a few hours, I declared Paris as my favourite city. At first sight, Paris looked amazing with the old buildings, narrow streets and crazy traffic. I was definitely going to come back to the city I have fallen in love with at first sight as soon as I could. It was magical and I felt so at home as if I had been here before. I loved the buildings, the people and the language, though it was very expensive.

I arrived at my hotel and was greeted warmly by the reception staff. I was even assisted with my luggage. My room was small and quaint with a window looking out to an alley. I unpacked Cardboard Paul and left him on the bed resting whilst I wandered the streets of Paris to find somewhere to eat. I pinched myself because I finally arrived in the one place I always wanted to visit.

I found a typical Parisian restaurant with chairs and tables set outside on the sidewalk. I walked in and ordered a small pizza and glass of wine in very basic French. I was there in Paris sitting at a French restaurant drinking wine but had no one to share it with. Although I certainly missed my darling Paul, I was also very happy to just be there.

I wandered back to the hotel and found a little supermarket up the road that stocked fresh food and snacks. I settled in for the night and sat up in bed watching one of my favourite shows *Death in Paradise* in French. Although I couldn't understand much, it was nice just to hear the French language and accent.

Day 2 – Getting Lost in Paris

*A*lyssa, my travel agent, had booked for me a tour of Versailles in the morning and I had to meet my tour group at Invalides train station. I was up early for my second day in the beautiful city and felt very excited. I walked downstairs and asked the concierge for the best way to travel to my destination. He suggested to take the bus instead of a taxi – that decision was probably not the better of the two options. He provided me with a map and directions. With Cardboard Paul in his calico bag over one shoulder and my handbag in the other, I hit the streets of Paris.

It was really early as I had to be at the pickup point by 8.30 am. I headed for the bus stop and waited and waited. It didn't look as though my bus was coming anytime soon and time was ticking away to get to the collection spot. I looked at my map of Paris and determined that I could walk to Invalides station, which in hindsight probably wasn't one of my better decisions considering the map and all the streets signs were written in French. My understanding of French was very limited at the best of times.

I kept walking thinking I was going in the right direction, looking at my map and getting totally confused and lost. I finally realised that I wasn't going to meet with my tour in time, so I just let it go and continued walking. I had been walking for a few hours and was getting hungry, so I found a nice little café, ordered a coffee and croissant, and sat down just watching the world go by. The sun was out and the air was warming up – it was going to be a beautiful day.

After filling my body with food, I started to walk and admire the amazing buildings, and just feeling the energy of the city. In the end, I put my map away and just wandered around. I found myself in the fashion district – it just so happened to be Fashion Week, so there were beautiful people everywhere. I kept walking, not knowing where I was going, I just followed my instincts.

I stumbled upon a beautiful garden, Jardin des Tuileries, and took an opportunity to rest and take Cardboard Paul out for a stroll and some photos. After plenty of photos, I looked around and up and saw what I came to Paris for. The Eiffel Tower in all her glory was standing in my sight. Overcome with emotion, I burst into tears. It was so overwhelming, my lifelong wish to visit Paris and the Eiffel Tower was now real. Again, I thought about how I was sharing this moment with Cardboard Paul instead of the real Paul.

Keeping the tower in sight, I started walking towards it. On the way, I had to use the toilet, so I paid €2 to go in the garden's public toilets – at least they were clean. I was off on a mission heading towards the tower. It was heating up into a beautiful, warm day in Paris. I walked past Place de la Concorde, over and along the river Seine, and past Invalides station where I was supposed to be hours earlier. I walked past the museum district and into the gardens where the Eiffel Tower stood. There were tourists everywhere and people lining up to go into the tower. I was not interested in queuing up for hours in the heat to walk up the tower, it was enough just to be in the area.

I wandered around the gardens and found a perfect spot to take photos of Cardboard Paul and me with the Eiffel Tower as the backdrop. How many other cardboard cut-outs can say that they have travelled around the world and visited the Eiffel Tower? I also took videos and uploaded them on Facebook under my *#tripofalifetime* blog.

There were plenty of souvenir sellers pushing their wares and I just politely said, 'No, thanks.' I wandered back towards my hotel along the Seine, hoping I was heading in the right direction. I backtracked the way I had come and walked past Place de la Concorde again and down little streets that meandered through Paris. I walked past the Ritz Paris and was reminded of that fateful day when we lost Princess Diana. On my travels, I also walked past the tunnel that she was killed in. There was a monument erected in honour of her memory.

I walked for a few more blocks and finally found the Avenue des Champs-Élysées and knew I was heading in the right direction. When I looked back at the map and where I was walking, I realised that I had walked in the opposite direction of where I was supposed to go and there was a more direct path. Despite getting lost in Paris, I was loving it.

7. Paris

On my walks, I found so many black and silver MINIs that I gave up counting, but I knew Paul was walking beside me. Once I arrived at the top end of the avenue near Arc de Triomphe, there was a huge canopy with the words 'PAUL' written on it. How many more signs was I going to see to know that he was travelling with me? PAUL was a popular bakery that offered freshly baked bread and pastries. I wandered into the shop and waited as it was packed with other customers. I decided on *le sandwich mixte* – a long baguette with ham and cheese – as well as a few macaroons and lemon tartlet, which would be my dinner for that evening.

It was still early in the afternoon and I headed out onto the streets again to pick up my tickets for the bus and river tours. As it was Fashion Week, there were some very interesting people in town. I walked down towards the Louvre Museum, and after my huge walk in the morning, I was becoming very familiar with the streets and the lay of the land, plus I had Google Maps giving me directions, just in case I wandered off the path again.

I headed down Saint-Honoré Street, passing through many shop windows displayed with some very weird mannequins. There were certainly some interesting outfits on display. I saw a shop that had thigh-high boots that glittered like small mirrored glass. I certainly couldn't see myself walking in something like that.

I was wandering back to the hotel with tickets in hand and saw this young woman walking in front of me with the most bizarre outfit on. I took a photo as I was sure no one back home would have believed me. A lovely French gentleman walked beside me and commented something in French. I said to him, '*Pardon, je suis Australianne, parlé vous Anglais?*' – which meant, 'I'm sorry, I'm Australian, do you speak English?'

He said, '*Oui*,' and started speaking English with the gorgeous French accent. He made a very unflattering comment about how the young lady was dressed up and commented that we both looked much better than her. I was not sure who was flirting with whom, but it was fun and he was so handsome. We bid farewell to each other and walked in our own directions.

Before I headed up to my room, I called into the petite supermarket near the hotel to stock up on some snacks. It was starting to get dark by the time I arrived back in my room and I settled in for the night, feasting on the baguette I had purchased from PAUL and finished off with a vanilla macaroon. I was happy and content and felt I could live in Paris if I had a chance, although it was an extremely expensive city to live in.

I had walked over 35,600 steps, had blisters on my blisters, and didn't even wonder why I was feeling exhausted. I pulled Cardboard Paul out of his bag, stood him up in the corner, and I laid on the bed exhausted.

Day 3 – Exploring Paris

I was up early again this morning and looked out the window to see a very overcast day with possible rain. I was looking forward to today as I was jumping on the Big Bus tour of Paris, which meant sitting instead of walking. I was certainly keeping fit on this tour. I climbed into the bus which was parked near Arc de Triomphe and sat inside instead of upstairs in the open, as it was wet and raining. On the bus, there were complimentary headphones and rain ponchos. I had my own headphones due to the issues I was having with infected ears. I grabbed a rain poncho for Cardboard Paul just in case he was going to get wet.

I highly recommend jumping on the Big Bus tour or anything similar when visiting a city, as it gives you a great overview of the iconic sites and ideas of where to explore further. Our journey on the Big Bus began by tackling the crazy traffic in the roundabout of Arc de Triomphe, Place Charles de Gaulle, and down Avenue des Champs-Élysées, past the Grand Palais on Avenue Winston Churchill, over the Seine, and then past Invalides station. Realising how far off the track I was the day before, I totally loved getting lost in Paris, as it was well worth exploring.

I was immersing myself in the Paris vibe and had been craving *soupe à l oignon français* – French onion soup. I found a petite café and sat down to a bowl of onion soup, red wine and topped it off with a light gâteau. I was fortunate that majority of people in Paris spoke English – usually after you make an attempt to speak French first.

Whilst travelling around this magnificent city, I met a mother and daughter from Melbourne on the bus sitting behind me. They had caught the train from London to Paris for the day. I was telling them the story of travelling with Cardboard Paul and they were amazed that I was travelling alone and honouring his memory.

Day 4 – Relaxing in Paris

I was up early and walked down to the Louvre again hoping to visit this famous museum, but I wasn't the only tourist with the same idea as the crowds were starting to build. I decided to find a place and sit down for some breakfast instead. I found this quaint coffee shop not far from the Louvre and ordered a *croque monsieur* – toasted ham and cheese sandwich – and a latte. The croque monsieur was huge and very yummy.

After my big breakfast, I did some window shopping on my way back to the Louvre and the crowds had doubled in size. The line to the entrance was now snaking its way around, filling up far too quickly. The police and army presence were also evident as Paris was on high alert.

Instead of walking all the way back to the hotel, I went to catch the Big Bus. Halfway through our journey, we had to change buses due to a flat tyre – what was it with buses breaking down, especially with flat tyres? This was the third bus on my trip that had some kind of issue.

We couldn't go down Champs-Élysées as the street was closed for a L'Oréal fashion show. There were police everywhere and security was tight and high. I heard on the news later that evening that there had been an incident in Marseille with two women being killed. I was watching the news on television and trying to understand what they were saying. I took a video of the news footage and then tried to translate it to English to fathom what was going on.

I decided to stay in for dinner and wandered downstairs to the bar and ordered a club sandwich, it was scrumptious and went down really well with a bottle of red wine that I had purchased from the petite supermarket.

I had one more day in this magnificent city and wanted to make the most of it, so I was in bed early.

Day 5 – Final Day in Paris

It was a beautiful day and the Parisians were surprised by the warm weather. We had a few days of overcast with Sunday raining all day but it didn't deter the tourists from lining up for the Louvre Museum, Arc de Triomphe and every other tourist attraction in Paris.

I was up early and went downstairs for breakfast in the hotel restaurant. It was a smorgasbord of different types of food and I went for the basic scrambled eggs and bacon. The food in Paris tasted so different to anywhere else I had been as it was so fresh and tasty. I topped the meal off with a nice cup of black tea and headed out the door for another fun-filled day of exploring.

I was back on the Big Bus and decided to explore both the red and blue sections of the tour which took me out past Moulin Rouge – it was much smaller than I expected. I was interested in stopping at Sacré-Cœur Basilica but the hike from the bus was uphill and I just didn't have the energy to tackle much walking that day.

When we stopped at the Notre-Dame Cathedral, I went inside to explore this magnificent church. The queues to enter the church were not that long, so I lined up with all the other tourists and went in the large doors. As soon as I entered the church, I got chills. It was amazing and very emotional. I stopped and lit a candle for Paul and Mum and then walked around taking videos of the interiors of the church. The stained-glass windows were absolutely stunning. On my way out of the church, I called by the gift shop and purchased some rosary beads for Mum.

7. Paris

After my tour of the church, I headed back to the bus stop and jumped on again until I reached near the Louvre. I stepped off the bus and wandered towards the shops to see if I could find a toilet. In Paris, the restrooms were not the easiest to find and you had to pay an entrance fee. I found a little café and asked where the toilets were and then sat down for a coffee and croissant. After my snack, I stopped by a tourist shop to find a French beret. I bought one in navy blue and also found some fridge magnets for Pauline.

I was back on the bus and took in all the monuments and attractions as we slowly meandered back up to Arc de Triomphe, which was my stop to get off and head back to the hotel. I was now becoming very familiar with this city and loved every minute of it.

It was my last night in this beautiful, magical city. I was going to miss it, but I promised to return. The next day, I was heading off on the next leg of my awesome *#tripofalifetime* to London via train. It would be the start of a 20-day tour of the best of the British Isles. Cardboard Paul was going to make many more appearances as he travelled with me. I finally put his wet weather gear – the poncho – on him just in case we had bad weather on the next part of our journey.

During this whole journey, I was asking my spiritual guides for direction and clarity. What was I doing at home? Work was not feeling right, I felt stalled and was going nowhere. I needed clarity, I needed direction, and I felt lost, especially around my career. I had booked meeting rooms in Hawthorn to run some workshops, and in the end, I cancelled the space as it wasn't feeling right. I was now getting in touch with the real me and following my intuition. I didn't know where I was heading in my business or career, but I knew that during this time away, the answers would eventually come.

I will visit Paris again as I felt at home there. It gave me the incentive to take up French lessons again. I hope that when I did return, I would be able to converse fluently with the locals. I have the ability to decipher the written words most of the time, but I have trouble with the spoken words.

People who have visited Paris before told me that the city was dirty and the people were rude and arrogant. My impression was the complete opposite where I found the people friendly and they spoke English. The city was much cleaner than New York and San Francisco.

8
London

Paris to London

*A*s my train wasn't leaving until early afternoon, I was able to have a bit of a sleep in and leisurely make my way downstairs for breakfast. Cardboard Paul was tucked snuggly in my case ready for our journey to London.

I booked a taxi through the hotel concierge to get to the station. I bid farewell to the reception staff with '*merci beaucoup, au revoir*' and headed to the station. I stared out the window just watching the beautiful buildings go by and the odd monument or two as we drove towards Gare du Nord.

I alighted from the taxi and paid the driver, then proceeded to lug my heavy suitcase into the station. I remembered an advice a friend had given me and headed upstairs to the information counter. I handed over a piece of paper which had my ticket information, and they pointed me in the right direction. I queued up where I had to go through security. I flashed my ticket and passport, lifted my heavy suitcase and hand luggage onto the security belt to go through the screens, and then lifted it off on the other end. I made a note to myself that on my next travels, especially if I was travelling by land, to pack much lighter. It then made me think about how much more luggage I was carrying – physically, mentally and emotionally. Many of us walk around with this heavy load and don't necessarily acknowledge it. I was grateful that during this journey, I was really getting to know the real me, although I was still questioning where I was heading career-wise once I arrived home.

We were finally able to board the train, which was no mean feat when lugging over 30 kg of luggage. To get into the train there was a large step up. I threw in my large suitcase first, then my smaller carry-on before stepping up into the train myself. I found a spot for my large suitcase and proceeded to find my seat. I was just getting settled when someone came up and said, 'I think you are in my seat.' I looked at my paperwork and then looked at her blankly and asked if the seat numbers were the same in each carriage. She replied with a 'yes'. I just assumed that the seats were numbered from 1 to 100, when in fact, the same series of numbers repeated themselves but had a letter in front of them to differentiate the carriages. Another lesson for me was not to follow others, always check my tickets and the signage outside of the train.

I was in the right seat just in the wrong carriage. I was lucky that my seat was only two carriages down the train. Instead of lugging my suitcase in and out of the carriage, I left it where it was as it was not that far from where I was sitting. I had to drag my carry-on, laptop bag and handbag through the two carriages with a narrow walkway and other passengers moving around. It was a nightmare, but I persisted and finally found my seat. I collapsed in the seat, hot, bothered and very frustrated.

I had the window seat so I was hoping no one was going to sit beside me, but as the train was fairly full, that was not going to be the case. A tall, young-ish Englishman sat beside me. He was not the talkative type and didn't really acknowledge me, so I just sat and stared out the window, headphones on and listening to my music and writing notes. My English companion was also an armrest hog as he decided that he would take up all the space and make me feel cramped. What is it with Aussies who are happy to chat? I think we are friendly – a comment that was made constantly in the USA. Are people so paranoid now that they won't talk to each other, or is it just pure rudeness?

The sun was shining, warming up my face, and the countryside whizzed by as the train headed towards London. I felt really excited as I was looking forward to meeting new people on this next tour. As we headed towards the tunnel, the train stopped and an announcement was made that they had stopped for security measures. I was not sure what it was but we were only delayed for about fifteen minutes, after which we went speeding through the tunnel. Not long after entering the tunnel, I felt tired and dropped off into a deep sleep. I don't know how long I was out, but it felt weird as I have never done that before, it was like going into surgery and being anesthetised.

8. London

The train ride was very smooth and quick but the seating was not so comfortable. I found travelling backwards on the train very uncomfortable and weird. I do prefer to travel facing forward, as it feels normal.

We finally arrived at St Pancras International train station in London. I waited until all the passengers had alighted and then I weaved my way through the carriages and heaved my luggage down the large step. I sympathised with the elderly man who had a walker and looked like he was struggling. I asked him if he was all right or needed help. He thanked me and said he was fine. I followed the others through the station and was really surprised that I didn't have to go through any security or show my passport. There was a presence of custom officers, but no passenger was approached by them. I walked further through the station looking at the signs and was happy that I could actually read them. I found where I needed to catch a taxi to my next accommodation. I stepped into a London taxi and was fascinated by them.

The sun was shining and warming up, which I thought was unusual as London was supposed to always be grey and rainy. Nevertheless, I welcomed the beautiful weather.

The cabbie asked me where I was from and what I was doing. I told him about Cardboard Paul and my travels so far. He couldn't believe it and thought I was very brave to travel around the world by myself.

We arrived at my hotel and I thanked the driver and walked towards the hotel reception to check in. This hotel was very new and upmarket. I know that the room rate per night was very expensive, but this is where the tour started. I was given my room key and escorted up to my room by the porter.

My room was massive and had an amazing feature wall that was lit up with the word 'London' in blue. It took me a while to work out how to turn it off as I didn't particularly want it lit up during the night whilst I was trying to sleep. The backlit feature wall was an opportunity to take some selfies with Cardboard Paul, so I took a few and posted them up on the *Conversations with Paul* Facebook page.

In the bathroom was a set of scales and I was keen to see how much I weighed. I was pleasantly surprised at the number as I had lost at least 8 kg. This travelling was very good for my fitness and health.

I hit the bed early and was excited to start my next tour and meet my fellow tour family.

Day 1 – Walking Around London

This was the first day of the tour, but unlike the USA tour, I actually didn't get to meet the rest of the tour group until the third day, so the timings of the tour were deceiving.

I was given a welcome envelope and instructions of where to meet the Globus tour coordinator. I found him, Tim, sitting in the reception area and I introduced myself. He gave me an update as to what was happening the next day and provided me with a map and tips on where to go and directions to get back to the hotel.

With my map in hand, I ventured out into the mild day with the sun shining, which again, I found unusual for London. I started to walk, and just around the corner, I spotted Big Ben. I walked on the Westminster Bridge across River Thames and noticed that they had installed large bollards beside the pathway. I assumed this was a precaution to stop cars from mowing down pedestrians, which had occurred in early June 2017 on the London Bridge where a van deliberately rammed into people, and the assailants jumped out of the vehicle and started stabbing innocent people. It was extremely sad that our world and famous places had to put systems and precautions in place to protect the people.

As I walked around the city of London taking photos of Big Ben, Houses of Parliament and other London landmarks amongst the throng of tourists, I had to stop and pinch myself. I did a happy scream in my head as I couldn't believe I was standing here in London. I felt at home walking around the streets of London, as though I had been there before, just not in this lifetime.

8. London

On my walk, I saw iconic symbols of London, such as the red double-decker buses, red telephone boxes and even the blue police telephone box which was no longer in use. I just thought it looked like Doctor Who's flying TARDIS was placed on the side of the River Thames. I was expecting it to disappear at any moment.

Walking along the River Thames, I wandered through the beautiful Whitehall Gardens that had large trees and paths lined with pebbles. There was also the Royal Horse Guards Hotel which faced the gardens. I loved the architecture of the building as it looked like a French château. There was construction in the area and a constant banging could be heard coming from the river's edge.

I headed back towards my hotel as it was getting late and I walked past the Old Vic – an old theatre with plenty of history. On the corner of where my hotel was, there was a great souvenir shop that I wandered into. I found these cute little T-shirts with a furry Queen's guard on the front.

I bought two of them, one for my grandniece and the other for my step-grandson. I also bought some other souvenirs for the family, as well as another fridge magnet for my tour buddy Pauline. My collection of fridge magnets for Pauline was expanding and I had only just started the Great Britain and Ireland tour.

I arrived back into my room, put away all my souvenirs and wandered down into the hotel restaurant for dinner. It was rather busy in the restaurant, so I ordered something light and sat at a small coffee table with a glass of wine in hand. Whilst I was waiting for my meal, there was a strange man staring at me which made me feel uncomfortable.

I was not sure if he was there to pickup anyone, but I certainly was not in the market and it was just creepy. I finished my meal and drink ever so quickly, walked back up to my room for a good night's sleep and prepared for my big day in the morning.

Day 2 – London Tour

This morning I had a quick bite to eat in the hotel restaurant before our tour began. I felt excited as I was going to meet new people.

Tim, the Globus tour coordinator, was in the reception area and advised that our tour coach was on the way, apologising for its late arrival. The coach had been caught in early morning traffic and took some time to arrive. Whilst we were waiting, a group started to gather and chat about the different tours. Some of us were on the same tour, so we introduced ourselves, giving a brief background of where we were from.

The coach finally arrived, our tour group hopped onto the coach and grabbed our seats for our tour around London. There were twenty-six people on this tour, with Simon as our tour guide, and Steve, our coach driver. Simon was a good looking Irishman in his early thirties with an awesome accent, while Steve was from Wales and in his late fifties. They made a great team considering that this was their first tour together.

On our morning sightseeing tour, we were privileged to have a local tour guide named Robert. He knew his stuff and was full of stories about the famous landmarks we were visiting or driving past; House of Parliament, Big Ben beside River Thames, Westminster Abbey, and Whitehall's mounted horse guards, the Prime Minister's residence at Downing Street, Piccadilly Circus and Buckingham Palace.

Our first stop was St Paul's Cathedral where we had our bags checked prior to entering this massive cathedral. Walking up the stairs I stopped to look back, remembering Princess Diana walking up those steps prior to marrying Prince Charles. The Cathedral has had its fair share of drama with the Great Fire of London destroying the Old St Paul's Cathedral, and then being struck by bombs in the Blitz in 1940 and 1941.

The building was massive and very impressive. When I walked deeper into the cathedral, I could sense this strange energy, possibly because of the crypt inside the cathedral. The crypt housed tombs of some famous people, including a huge memorial on the cathedral floor for the Duke of Wellington. After touring the depths of the cathedral, we headed back outside into the sunshine and onto our coach for our next stop, Buckingham Palace.

Whilst on our way to Buckingham Palace, Robert was telling us about the perfect spot to see the palace and the Changing of the Guard. People usually gathered right in front of the palace gates, but we were on a side street in front of the big gates and had the perfect position to see the ceremonial pageantry.

I was walking through the gardens, following the group towards this perfect spot when the lovely Louise from Canada walked up beside me and asked if I was happy to buddy up with her. I agreed, of course, as it was lovely to meet another like-minded person that I could share these moments with.

Whilst the group found their perfect position and waited for the guards to march by, I crossed the road, pulled out Cardboard Paul and started taking selfies. Louise asked if I wanted a photo from a distance to include the gardens and the palace as a backdrop and, of course, I said 'yes'. I now had my second willing photographer for this part of the journey.

We took plenty of photos with Cardboard Paul in the garden with Buckingham Palace as the backdrop. Again, I had to pinch myself. After our photo session, we wandered back to where the others were standing and the crowds were getting bigger. There was a big police presence in the area, a policewoman was shouting at tourists telling them to get off the road and not to climb up on barriers and fences. I was standing next to Gerard, another tour member from Texas, and we were entertained by the policewoman and the antics of the crowd. We were having a good laugh and chatting away.

In the background, we could hear the band tuning their instruments, it was time for them to start the parade. We were in a prime position to watch the parade; first came the military band marching in full regalia, fluffy black helmets and red jackets, then came the guards in uniform marching behind them. It was spectacular and surreal.

There I was in front of Buckingham Palace at this moment in time experiencing this amazing journey with a cardboard cut-out of Paul, but I wished Paul was there with me in person.

The next stop on our tour was Windsor Castle. The coach pulled into the car park, the group alighted and walked casually through the town of Windsor via the beautiful old train station and quaint shops. Robert led us through the cobbled streets leading in and out of Windsor Castle. On our way into the castle we passed the gift shop and I made a mental note to pop in there after the tour.

Robert told us about the Union Flag that was flying at the time and advised that the Queen was not in residence. If the Royal Standard Flag was flying, then it meant that the Queen was there. The Queen was apparently up in Balmoral Castle, Scotland at the time.

We walked through the amazing Windsor Castle gardens which were laid out in 2002 for the Queen's Golden Jubilee, and later upgraded. The grass and shrubbery were green and lush.

Our first stop inside the castle was Queen Mary's Dolls' House which was amazing and not what I was expecting. This dollhouse was huge and behind a glass case with multiple rooms and miniature furniture. There was also a display of different dolls and their outfits, along with other types of toys.

After wandering around the dollhouse, we proceeded towards the State Apartments. When entering these rooms, I could feel the energy changing with every room I entered. When I entered into the King's bedroom, I felt as though someone was trying to stop me, as if I was being blocked from entering. I was starting to feel dizzy and sick, and was nearly knocked off my feet. I knew it wasn't me but some spirit that was hanging around making its presence and intentions felt.

This was the case in many of the rooms that I entered. I could feel the coolness in the air and the changing frequencies as I walked from one room to another. I am sure there were a few old kings still hanging around the palace that hadn't moved on. After walking through many of the rooms, I felt a presence that seemed familiar and I asked whose room it was, and the reply was King Henry VIII. This was my first encounter with Henry and not my last.

After exploring the expansive rooms in the State Apartments, I wandered back out into the gardens with Louise and took the opportunity to take more photos with Cardboard Paul. There was a guard standing near a guard box holding a heavy machine gun. I stood beside him with Cardboard Paul for a great photo together. The guard just stood there with his head facing straight forward and his face expressionless. I wondered if he thought, 'What are these two up to?'

We walked into an ornate church and saw the tombs of Queen Mother and King George. After our photo shoot, we walked towards the coach, stopping by the Windsor Castle courtyard souvenir shop. I picked up a book on Windsor Castle, toffees and a hessian bag with the castle's logo on it.

Once our tour group was back and accounted for on the coach, we headed back to the hotel through Windsor and the London suburbs.

In the evening, I had a taste of the London experience with dinner at a traditional London pub with other tourists. I sat on a table with people from New Zealand, America and Australia, some of whom were from a different tour group. The pub was quaint but very loud. Our table was upstairs, so I had to climb up a spiral staircase. Thankfully, I had flat shoes and not high heels on.

After our three course meal, and of course, a few beers, our group was then ushered back onto the coach and down to the River Thames where we went on our river cruise. Our tour guide for the evening was Robert from earlier that day. I found a spot on the top deck and braved the cold wind to have some amazing views, including that of a beautiful full moon. The city was striking at night with all the different lights on the different iconic buildings and bridges.

It was an amazing day and I felt extremely grateful that I had the opportunity to have these wonderful experiences, even though by myself, but I knew Paul was with me in spirit – and also in cardboard.

9
Great Britain

Day 3 – London – Oxford – Stratford-Upon-Avon – Warwick

We were finally on our full tour, with the group climbing on the coach and sitting down. As our tour only had twenty-six people, it was a nice small group and there were plenty of room on the coach to spread out.

We were formally introduced to our tour guide and coach driver, Simon and Steve. Simon's explanation of the coach seat rotation system was hilarious. Seeing how people were moved and taken out of their comfort zone was very interesting. Each day you had to move to a different seat moving clockwise, giving each passenger a different perspective, as well as the opportunity to sit with a different group of people.

Simon was upfront and laid out specific rules, including complaints relating to insignificant issues which I found refreshing, although this did not stop people from whinging to others in the group. Unless there was a major issue, he didn't want to know about it. I found it very fascinating to watch the dynamics of people in a group in this manner. Simon advised that this tour was for travelling and seeing – not a holiday to sit on the beach with a gin and tonic under the sun.

We started our tour by hitting the road, weaving through the streets and heavy traffic of London. On our way out of London, we passed by Grenfell Tower, the multi-story council housing that burnt down a few months before. It was devastating and sad to know that all those people had lost their lives due to shoddy construction work. I closed my eyes and sent my blessings to all those that lost their lives and to the families that were left to pick up the pieces.

The group that sat around me started to chat and we introduced ourselves. This was the first introduction to Cardboard Paul and the rest of the group were now starting to ask questions.

Travelling With Cardboard Paul

Our first stop, Hampton Court Palace, was historically owned and resided by King Henry VIII. It was situated along the River Thames, with breathtaking ornamental gardens, calm blue water and picturesque stone arch bridge in the distance.

As I was walking up to the residence, I felt the presence of King Henry VIII again, no doubt I picked him up from Windsor Castle and he decided he wanted to be with me. I told Louise that Henry was with us again and she just laughed. I said he just loved spending time with me, no doubt we had met in a previous lifetime. I asked Henry if he wanted to move on back home and he declined saying he was having more fun here in spirit, scaring those that could feel him. I did not feel scared, if anything, I loved his energy, which was larger than life and fun, something that I would have expected when he was alive – not forgetting that he had a terrible temper and manipulated people to get what he wanted, especially disposing of his wives. This was the young playful Henry that I encountered, prior to his injury from falling off a horse whilst jousting.

We had a stunning sunny day with blue skies and not too many clouds as we walked through the gardens. They were absolutely magnificent and the building's architecture was amazing. Our tour only included the gardens and not the actual building itself, which was disappointing. Nevertheless, I enjoyed walking through the gardens in the beautiful weather, imagining the days when King Henry VIII was around and how opulent this palace would have been.

We took photos of Cardboard Paul in the gardens with Louise as my new photographer. The group watched on and others started taking photos of us as well. The tour group was starting to get to know Cardboard Paul and his story.

These gardens were magnificent and spacious, it took us a while to walk around them. The group arrived at a side gate and we waited for someone to let us through, but it was locked and no one was coming. After waiting a while – and some muttering and the odd swearing – Simon walked back towards the house and asked what had happened.

9. Great Britain

Someone finally opened the gate, and instead of walking out of the gardens back to the coach, we were given a short tour of the house. As we walked through the palace, I was getting huge tingles – this place was haunted. I could see the spirits of children racing around the palace. Louise was also having a similar experience.

I certainly wanted to come back and visit this place again, as it was haunted and I was picking up on something. I made a mental note that if I was coming back to London, I would come back to Hampton Court Palace for a proper tour and perhaps bump into Henry again.

Our next stop was Runnymede, the site of the sealing of the Magna Carta. We drove in and out of the area without stopping, no doubt there was not much to see, despite being a significant part of history.

Our next port of call was a walking tour around the university city of Oxford. Harry Potter fans would have loved the displays in the windows as some of the buildings were used in the films. I loved Oxford as the energy was amazing, I was starting to really feel the places we were visiting and picking up on spirits.

The shops had some very funny displays of Harry Potter characters, including Dobby the House Elf, and the uniforms worn by the different houses. There was also a window dedicated to Paddington Bear, who I absolutely loved and was fortunate to have a stuffed version at home. Again, I made a mental note to come back and visit Oxford as we didn't have enough time to really explore this beautiful city.

We were on the coach again and heading to Stratford-upon-Avon, Shakespeare's birthplace. The coach pulled up in a car park beside Anne Hathaway's cottage. I put on some lippy for the photo shoot before we all piled out and crossed the road to have a group photo taken by a professional photographer with Anne Hathaway's house as the backdrop. Everyone found a spot to sit or stand and I pulled out Cardboard Paul for the group shot. I think a few people looked twice and was wondering what was going on and what was this cardboard cut-out.

All the buildings in Stratford-upon-Avon were built in the Tudor style. We were also able to see live performances of Shakespeare's works held in the courtyard behind his house.

As I was walking around Shakespeare's birthplace, I felt his presence and a calm and loving energy. I could see William himself writing from a spot and looking out the window, it was surreal.

When we moved to the back area, the energy changed, we were told that this area was leased out after Shakespeare's father had died. It was offered to weary travellers to make money. The energy seemed louder and angrier, as if someone was fighting. I was overcome by a headache and felt sick, but knew these feelings were not mine and I was picking up on someone else's energy.

The William Shakespeare tour also included a great souvenir shop with plenty of items related to his works for sale. I picked up a few magnets for Pauline and a small book of Shakespeare's quotes for Sarah.

Simon came up to me later and told me that an Indian couple were totally confused and didn't know what was going on with the cardboard person when we were having our group photo. I had to laugh and say that they will certainly get to know him soon enough.

After we settled back into our hotel that night, I had weird dreams and heard noises in the room. The next morning at breakfast, I mentioned this to Louise who had a similar experience.

To this day, I cannot remember the first night on the road or the hotel we stayed at, which is rather bizarre as I can remember most of the hotels and our nights, or have relied on notes that I made along my journey. No doubt I went travelling in an out-of-body experience somewhere else – perhaps meeting up with Henry again?

Day 4 – Warwick – York

We were up super early as we had a private tour of Warwick Castle – a medieval castle developed from a wooden fort – scheduled before the crowds came in. It was originally built by William the Conqueror in 1068. Warwick itself was the county town of Warwickshire, situated on a bend of the River Avon.

Walking through a stone archway and paved cobblestone, we walked past large shields and flags. At the height of the castle's period, they used to hang heads at the gate to deter visitors.

As we entered the castle, Simon gave us a history lesson. The people of that time were barbaric, and you could imagine this just by walking through the arch into the castle grounds, it gave me chills. We were introduced to our private tour guide Mark who was an encyclopaedia of information about Warwick Castle and the area. It was fascinating, and after our history lesson, we were left on our own to explore the castle and its grounds.

Warwick Castle was used as a stronghold until King James I granted it to Sir Fulke Greville in 1604. The Greville family converted it into a country house, and even became Earls of Warwick in 1759. Greville was later murdered by a discontented manservant, and his ghost was said to haunt the tower in which he lodged. In 1978, Warwick Castle was bought by the Tussauds Group and they later introduced wax portraits into the castle for the first time. Cardboard Paul and I had so much fun posing with portraits of royalty, even with King Henry VIII and all his wives. Room after room, there were different wax characters and we posed with most of them, including a young Winston Churchill and King George.

We wandered up to the tower and you could feel the coolness and a different energy. No doubt Sir Fulke Greville was still hanging around. On the wall was a number of picture frames that came to life, very much like the Harry Potter films. Each frame had different characters in them that became animated and told the story of Sir Fulke Greville's tragic murder. At first, I wasn't quite sure what was going on, but I stood there fascinated as I watched the story unfold. The story was very light and funny considering the darkness of the history. It was very entertaining and really cool, and not too scary for the kids that were watching.

We wandered some more around the castle and into the dungeon, which was dark, gloomy and cold, but also sold refreshments. Out into the beautiful sunshine, we explored the gardens and walked towards the jousting area, which was not yet open. After touring the gardens, we strolled back towards the coach and continued on to our next destination – York.

We arrived at York, a gorgeous quaint town with Tudor style buildings and narrow cobblestone alleyways. We walked down the narrow streets, one was called Shamble Street, where they brought animals to slaughter out in the open in the 1030's. Those days were long gone and have been replaced by small old world shops selling everything from food to gifts to tartan. There was one shop called 'The Shop That Must Not Be Named', although I was not sure what they sold.

I had a photo opportunity beside a very large, old, worn-out, stuffed grizzly bear who was very cute. I walked past a big black double-decker bus that offered ghost tours which sparked my interest. York also had this huge market that I gladly wandered around. I found this shop selling beautiful handmade leather handbags which I couldn't resist and bought a lovely red tote bag. Another little town to explore if I ever had the chance to return to this charming part of the world.

Our hotel for the night was the Redworth Hall Hotel in Durham which was an exquisite old-worldly dwelling with stunning gardens.

Simon suggested that we have an 'AA meeting', meaning that we get to know each other more personally. We commenced the evening with welcome drinks in the bar area and stood around chatting with each other and also to any other guests that were nearby. I met a lovely young couple that were at the hotel for an engagement party. We were ushered into the formal dining room for dinner, and Gail and Hans, who were also from my tour, decided to take matters into their own hands and welcomed us all. Everyone took it in turns to introduce themselves and give a brief explanation of their story.

I listened intently, trying to remember names and faces as each person had a turn. Louise and I were helping each other out, so that when we were back on the coach, we could remember our fellow travellers' names. When it was my turn, I stood up, introduced myself and then gave a brief explanation of my journey. I told everyone about my promise to Paul and how I was travelling the world with a cardboard cut-out of him. By this time, most of them have seen Cardboard Paul and knew a bit about the story after our group photo at Anne Hathaway's house. Those that were curious about Cardboard Paul finally heard the story behind him.

Needless to say, we had plenty of food, wine and laughs that evening. I was really enjoying the journey with these amazing people so far, and looked forward to getting to know more about them as we travelled on our tour.

Day 5 – York – Jedburgh – Abbotsford – Edinburgh

Again, I had weird dreams, saw clear visions and heard noises in my room. I woke up asking my spiritual guides again for clarity. On catching up with Louise over breakfast, she had a similar experience and heard the noises as well.

I was given the message by my spiritual guides that Dublin is my home and I will understand and gain clarity once I get there. I felt that Dublin was a very spiritual place as messages started to flow. The keyword for my journey was clarity, and I was certainly receiving that.

We were on the road again heading towards Edinburgh. My case was packed and I had Cardboard Paul safely tucked away in his calico bag ready for any photo opportunities. As we had plenty of vacant seats around us, Cardboard Paul had a whole row to himself to sit back and relax until our next destination.

We were heading towards Edinburgh and visited Hadrian's Wall on the way. Hadrian's Wall was exactly that, a long wall made of large blocks of stone which has deteriorated over time. It was starting to cool down and the wind was picking up, so getting out of the coach to see a stone wall wasn't my favourite thing to do. Needless to say, I was off the coach just to stretch my legs and went back into the warmth very quickly.

We had reached the border between England and Scotland. The coach stopped and we hopped out to have a photo opportunity, despite it being bitterly cold, and the wind fierce. I couldn't miss the opportunity to take a photo with Cardboard Paul, so I held onto Cardboard Paul tightly while Louise took a few photos.

Our next stop was Abbotsford House, the home of Sir Walter Scott, and lunch in the adjoining Ochiltree's Café. Once we finished our delicious lunch with nice glass of red, we headed next door to explore the incredible home of Sir Walter Scott, a renowned Scottish historical novelist, poet, playwright and historian. Scott was an obsessive collector of books, artefacts, weaponry and more, which adorned throughout the large home. When we walked into the main room, the weaponry and armoury were displayed on all the walls, and even the ceiling. The collection was massive and impressive.

Our two lovely volunteer tour guides showed us around the house and spoke of the amazing man that Scott was, as well as his expansive collection of works. Every room seemed to have wall to wall bookshelves, housing over 9,000 original books that Scott had collected during his time.

We had arrived at our hotel, the Principal Edinburgh, where we were staying for a few nights. The room was very spacious and had a huge queen size bed that was very comfortable. I laid Cardboard Paul out on the bed to stretch out and have a rest after our long day on the coach.

I had booked most of the additional extras on offer by the tour company, so tonight we were off to the *Spirit of Scotland Show* with highland dancers, bagpipes and the 'Ceremony of the Haggis'. We were greeted at the door by a very tall, gorgeous-looking Scotsman playing the bagpipes in full Scottish attire. Like everyone, we all wondered what he was actually wearing under his kilt.

We were shown our table, and the place was full of other tourists. We were very excited to see the show and listen to the beautiful Scottish music. Many of us were singing along to *The Bonnie Banks o' Loch Lomond* – 'O ye'll tak' the high road, and I'll tak' the low road, and I'll be in Scotland a'fore ye'. There was much clapping and stamping to the bagpipes and accordion with audience participation. There was also the 'Ceremony of the Haggis' whereby plates of haggis were placed on the table in front of us. I am not really keen on trying new foods, so I declined on trying the haggis, but there were a few in our group that did try it. It was such a grand night being immersed in the Scottish culture.

It had been a long day and I was extremely happy to jump into bed for a good night's sleep. Beside the bed were two biscuits, but these were not your usual, everyday biscuit. They were wrapped in thin silver and red tinfoil. When I unfolded the tinfoil, a dome chocolate biscuit revealed itself, which reminded me of a chocolate royal, and the marshmallow just melted in your mouth. It was so delicious and went down well with a hot cup of tea.

Day 6 – Edinburgh

Today we were off on a morning city sightseeing tour of Edinburgh with Simon. Steve, our normal coach driver, was off for a few days to rest so we had a different driver. We travelled around the narrow streets, and all the buildings looked similar in a very brown, greyish colour. We made our way up to Edinburgh Castle and walked the steep incline to where we had to queue for a bag check prior to walking into the castle walls.

Edinburgh Castle sat on top of a rock and overlooked the city with impressive views. Louise and I wandered into the castle and instantly felt the energy change. As we wandered through the castle, the walls were full of armoury and paintings dating back centuries of past residents that lived in the castle. Mary, Queen of Scots, gave birth to James VI in this palace in 1566. I couldn't imagine what it was like to give birth in a cold, dark, damp atmosphere in that era, especially with no modern electricity, heating or medical equipment.

We were back in the courtyard and had a perfect photo opportunity with Cardboard Paul posing in front of the tall, black guard box. Unfortunately, there was no guard present at that time. I had the odd look from fellow tourists, but no one came up and asked about Cardboard Paul.

Our next stop was exploring the Scottish Crown Jewels, also known as the Honours of Scotland, displayed in the Crown Room. The jewels included the crown, sceptre and Sword of State. I learnt about the turbulent past of the jewels, whereby they were kept hidden from Cromwell's Parliamentarian army, and later locked in a chest and sealed away after the Treaty of Union between England and Scotland.

After viewing the Scottish Crown Jewels, we strolled down to St Margaret's Chapel. The chapel was built around 1130 by David I and dedicated to his mother, Queen Margaret. As we were walking out, we stopped near a large cannon in the Castle Esplanade.

I went into meditation and asked any souls that were connected with the castle if they wanted to move on back home. I had quite a few souls wanting to move on, and I was able to guide them. The energy changed and felt much lighter. Louise agreed and felt much lighter and less emotional after her experience with a flashback from a past life.

The next stop on our itinerary was Holyrood Palace, the official residence of Queen Elizabeth II in Scotland. Located at the opposite end to Edinburgh Castle, Holyrood Palace has served as the principal residence of Scottish monarchs since the 16th century, and is a setting for state occasions and official entertaining.

9. Great Britain

We were able to tour the historic apartments of Mary, Queen of Scots and the State Apartments which did not disappoint with the magnificent ornate rooms.

As we entered the estate through the large iron gates and past the ornate water fountain, there was a strong smell of roast beef which made me feel hungry.

Once inside, I walked through the state rooms and took the odd photo. Then one of the security guards pointed out to me that there was no photography allowed – *oops*, I didn't read that sign, I was too busy looking at the ornate furnishings. I was able to keep the photo of the red thrones with the royal crests on them. Luckily, my phone wasn't taken off me.

The gardens in the palace were expansive and stunning. It was very peaceful walking through the gardens. It was mentioned by one of the tour guides that Princess Anne often stays in the apartments while away from the palace. On our walk, we went through the medieval abbey that is now ruined, although there are parts of the building still intact.

Back at our hotel we had a few hours of free time before our next excursion later that evening. Louise and I went into town looking for a chemist as Louise was getting a cold and my arthritis was starting to play up. We found this very large health food shop where I found some Devil's Claw that was used to treat arthritis.

I found that it helped and kept the pain down to a minimum. Louise managed to find something for her cold as well. We then had a good look around all the shops where nearly every window had some tartan pattern on display.

After our tour around the shops in Edinburgh, we called back into the hotel for a well-earned coffee and cake before our big night out. We were off to visit the Royal Yacht Britannia before dinner.

The Royal Yacht Britannia, was the Queen's former floating palace for over forty years from 1954 until 1997. It was now berthed in Edinburgh and just happened to be connected to a large shopping centre. The yacht was extremely impressive and luxurious, no doubt fit for the royal family and definitely out of my league.

As we strolled around the yacht, it was amazing to have a look into the lives of the royal family and how they spent their time on board. On the walls, lovely personal photos of the royal family were displayed. The yacht was very long, with many levels and rooms.

The dining room where they entertained many guests over the years had a very long dining room table, this table was massive and the place setting was laid out on display – it looked like a dinner function was about to begin.

Walking through the different areas, there were lounge rooms and even the bedrooms of both the Queen and Prince Philip. Interestingly, they both had separate rooms with king-size single beds. Prince Charles and Princess Diana spent their honeymoon on board and it was good to see that they had a double bed in their room. The yacht also had a garage on board that housed a Rolls-Royce Phantom V which was actually still on board!

My favourite room on board was the family room towards the back of the yacht, which a beautiful teak-lined room was furnished with heavy cane furniture and a very comfortable couch. Apparently, this room was one of the Queen's favourite spaces on board and you could see why, as it felt relaxed, peaceful and had some nice views.

After our tour of the yacht, we went down the gangplank outside in front of the yacht and I had a photo opportunity with a metal statue sailor with a big cheeky smile on his face – I didn't tell Cardboard Paul about this. After our tour we headed to an Italian restaurant for a great meal and conversation over a few wines.

Day 7 – Edinburgh – St Andrews – Pitlochry – Culloden – Inverness

Our time in Edinburgh was over and we were on the road again heading towards Inverness. Our first stop was St Andrews Links, the 'Home of Golf'.

Founded in 1843, it was one of the oldest golf courses in the world. Although I was not into golf, the scenery was spectacular with the course overlooking the North Sea from St Andrews Bay. It was bitterly cold and windy, so brisk walking was the only way to go. We wandered into St Andrews golf shop as Louise was looking for some golfing souvenir for her son. Everything we picked up was expensive, although Louise was able to find a wooden golf cover as a present for her son.

Our next stop was Culloden Battlefield. Earlier on the bus, Simon gave us a history lesson on the Battle of Culloden and Bonnie Prince Charlie, so we knew what to expect. The Culloden Battlefield was the site of the last battle to take place on British soil. On 16th of April, 1746, Bonnie Prince Charlie and his army of 5,000 Jacobite Highlanders faced off against the Duke of Cumberland and 9,000 Hanoverian government troops. As I walked through the display centre and listened to the audio, it was very confronting to hear and see what had happened during the battle.

Louise and I walked out into the field, and instantly, I could feel the energy. I was starting to feel the familiar dizziness and headaches. I was also getting the odd flashback and could sense those on the battlefield. The feelings of being frightened, scared and lost were overwhelming. I felt very sad and emotional. Whilst walking through the fields and between all the red and blue flags, I was asking those souls that were stuck there if they wanted to return home. In the middle of the field, I closed my eyes and directed those souls to their own guides and angels, and they were swiftly returned home. I felt calm and happy knowing that those souls stuck in this memory for centuries were now free.

We had finally reached our accommodation for the evening, the Columbia Hotel, Inverness. The room was tiny and very difficult to move around in. Our group made arrangements to meet in the bar for dinner and discuss our day.

That night I jumped into bed and immediately felt itchy all across my body and throughout the night. It was disgusting and I was definitely sharing my bed with bed bugs. The next morning at breakfast, I mentioned it to the group and they said that I should have complained to the hotel reception then and there and be moved. I said that it was far too late as the reception would have already been closed at that time. I complained to the hotel reception during check-out and the girl behind the counter started to argue with me, saying that it couldn't be the case as it was all new bedding. I told her I didn't know what it was, but it certainly made a meal out of me all night. When I met up with Simon on the bus, I told him about my conversation with the hotel reception and he couldn't believe it. I also mentioned it to Alyssa, my travel agent, who was keeping a dossier of the issues I was having on this *#tripofalifetime*.

Day 8 – Inverness – Fort William – Glasgow

*T*oday was going to be exciting as we were visiting the Loch Ness Centre and Exhibition.

Prior to arriving at Loch Ness, Simon informed us that the people at the Loch Ness Centre and Exhibition were going to search our bags and the coach! Everyone started to laugh and said, 'Well, we better hide all our weaponry and drugs.' It was too funny considering when we arrived at the exhibition it was such an understatement and letdown. I am not sure what I was expecting but it certainly didn't live up to the expectation I had in my head, it was far too cheesy. At least they had a yellow submarine out at the front.

Our next stop was Ben Nevis distillery to see the process of distilling whisky. Mary and Ben from USA were getting far too excited to the point where I think they nearly bought out the whole whisky shop.

9. Great Britain

Our tour began at the distillery and the smell was so overwhelming that it made me feel sick. I spent most of my time outside in the fresh air despite it raining. I had to stand on the edge near the doorway to keep dry. The smell took me back to the Nabisco days where Paul and I worked and when they were making Vita Brits, it had a similar disgusting, overpowering smell.

The rain was not stopping, and as we drove through the hills, the water was cascading down looking spectacular. It was freezing, raining and windy, and us, crazy people were heading out on a boat onto Loch Lomond. The scenery was spectacular and I huddled down undercover in some kind of warmth. My compatriots, the Aussies, decided to take a photo opportunity at the back of the boat and was nearly blown overboard. I certainly stayed undercover after that.

My highlight for the day was sitting in the bus, listening to Scottish music, watching Loch Ness go by, and heading to Loch Lomond with the appropriate song, *The Bonnie Banks o' Loch Lomond*. It was an amazing experience which filled my heart with gratitude and love.

We arrived in Glasgow, and prior to arriving at our hotel, we drove around the city with Simon providing us with a quick history lesson and pointing out the landmarks of the city. We arrived at the GoGlasgow Urban Hotel for the night in darkness. It was a quick check-in before heading to the dining room for dinner. My hotel room was very spacious and modern, which was one of the better hotel rooms I had stayed in.

Each morning at breakfast, we would compare our accommodation and make comments if it was suitable or not. Some tour buddies had specific requirements. I sympathised for Lisa and Marcie who required a walk-in shower, but unfortunately, most of our accommodations only had step-over baths. This time, the rooms Lisa and Marcie were offered were suitable for disabled people. It was nice to stay in a modern hotel with modern facilities, instead of the old world hotels that we were often staying at. Lisa was extremely happy that they had a walk-in shower in their room this time.

After dinner some of the group wandered out to have a look around, but I went straight up to my room and sat up in bed catching up with some television, updating *Conversations with Paul* on Facebook and chatting with my family.

Day 9 – Glasgow – Gretna Green – Lake District – Liverpool

I was really looking forward to today as we were headed to Liverpool, home to all things Beatles. I was a huge Beatles fan, especially Paul McCartney, and I was excited to visit the birthplace of the Beatles and the Beatles Story Exhibition. My suitcase was packed, ready to go and Cardboard Paul was packed in his calico bag ready for our big day.

The weather was overcast and started to rain with no signs of stopping. On this round of seat rotation, Louise and I were at the front of the bus, prime seats with an uninterrupted view out the front of the bus. Today was our biggest day in relation to the mileage of 383 kilometres in front of us.

Our first stop for the day was Gretna Green, a popular wedding destination made famous by its history whereby runaway brides were wedded in the blacksmiths' shops. By the time we arrived, it was pelting down rain. Everyone put on their rain jackets and hats, and pulled out umbrellas, although it didn't keep us dry as the rain was coming in sideways. We made a dash for the café so we could keep dry. Unfortunately, we were early and nothing much was opened yet. At least we were able to grab a coffee and snack before climbing back on the coach to go to our next stop.

The rain wasn't letting up, and what do you do when it is cold and wet outside? Put on a playlist of songs associated with rain. How many songs would you think were recorded about rain? Plenty, I can tell you. The best was *It's Raining Men*, which we were rocking away to as the scenery went by.

9. Great Britain

When we reached the Lake District, the water was cascading down the mountains with little waterfalls springing up everywhere. It was beautiful to watch the water tumbling down the green mountains.

Our next stop was a quaint little town, Grasmere in Lake District, which apparently was the wettest part of Scotland. It certainly lived up to its name and didn't let us down. Prior to alighting the bus, Simon gave us some key places to visit whilst walking around town. The rain was getting heavier and we walked beside the River Rothay which was flooded and flowing very quickly.

Our first stop in this town was St Oswald's Church. Grasmere has associations with the Lake Poets, one of whom, William Wordsworth, lived in Grasmere for fourteen years and called it 'the loveliest spot that man hath ever found.' Simon told us that in 1850, William died while out walking. He and his wife Mary, who died nine years later, have a simple tombstone in the graveyard of St Oswald's Church. The graveyard was flooded due to the heavy rain and there was mud everywhere. We couldn't really find Wordsworth's tombstone, so we walked through the graveyard past the church. Suddenly, we smelt gingerbread wafting through the air.

Our next stop happened to be the Grasmere Gingerbread Shop next door which was famous worldwide for its gingerbread. The recipe was created by Sarah Nelson sometime in the winter of 1854. She perfected a recipe for a new spicy-sweet sensation that she named simply Grasmere Gingerbread. The shop also sold homemade fudge – Lisa and I were huge lovers of fudge and would buy fudge whenever we came across some. I bought some gingerbread and homemade fudge to have later with a hot cuppa tea.

We were soaked, every item of clothing on me was drenched, and I was starting to feel really cold. Once back on the coach, I took my shoes and socks off trying to dry them out.

Our rain songs were still playing in the background as our trusty driver meandered through the tight laneways towards Liverpool. Windows were fogging up due to all of us being wet and our clothes soaking through.

We were back on the main highway again, and to keep us occupied and in the mood for our next stop, Simon started the Beatles quiz – thirty questions on all things Beatles. We also had the Beatles music playing in the background. The coach was rocking to us singing and clapping to all the Beatles tunes. I was in 7th Heaven, although some of the questions I was not sure of the answers.

We finally arrived at the Beatles Story Exhibition and the weather had changed for the better, we had some sunshine. As we walked through the door, *Magical Mystery Tour* was playing.

We grabbed our maps and audio player for our self-guided tour around the exhibition. There was so much to see while the Beatles music was blaring in the background. We had been walking through the exhibition and I looked at my watch and said to Louise that we only had an hour left before we were being picked up. We started to move through the exhibition faster and was a little disappointed that we didn't have anywhere enough time. We walked through the whole exhibition without really listening to the audio tour. We really needed more time. After the exhibition, we wandered into the souvenir shop and I picked up a few things – I could have bought so much more. I knew that if I was back in the area again, I would definitely spend more time at the exhibition.

We checked into Novotel Liverpool Centre, which again, was a nice modern hotel. After a quick change into dry clothes, a group of us were looking for somewhere to have dinner. We walked down the street and found a local pub not far from the hotel. I ordered the shepherd's pie, which was the best I have ever tasted, and it went down nicely with a glass of red. The Florida girls from the tour had frozen daiquiris and some nice pink drinks.

When I arrived back at my room, I hung my wet clothes in the bathroom trying to dry them out before the morning. My shoes, socks, gloves, jacket, jumpers, beanie, and even bra and undies were soaked through.

Day 10 – Liverpool – North Wales – Dublin

*T*oday was another exciting day as we were heading over the Irish Sea to Ireland.

Simon was starting to get sick with a cold and Louise wasn't shaking the cold that she developed in Edinburgh. It seemed that the whole coach was going to come down with something and I was making sure I wasn't going to get sick by keeping up with my Echinacea, zinc and vitamin C tablets daily. I had been fairly healthy throughout all my travels, so I didn't want to get any sickness in the little time I had left. We were at the halfway mark of our tour and the days were flying by. The end of our tour was creeping closer towards us and I had around fifteen days left before heading home. Sickness wasn't on my radar and I was steering clear of all those that were feeling under the weather.

We were back on the road again and I had moved halfway down the bus with Cardboard Paul having a seat to himself. The other tour buddies would ask how he was going and if he slept well. I just laughed and said he was doing fine.

Being halfway through our tour, my fellow tourists were becoming a little tour family and the camaraderie was lovely. Everyone was looking out for each other, especially for Larry and Elaine. Larry was battling cancer and his determination and stamina amazed everyone. I often asked Larry how he was going, and he always responded by smiling and saying, 'I am still breathing and have my two legs to walk, so going fine, thanks for asking.' There were many days that he wasn't able to join our group and needed to rest as much as he could. I would always ask Elaine how she was going, knowing too well what it was like to care for someone battling cancer.

We crossed the border into North Wales and called by Betws-y-Coed, a beautiful village with picturesque shops offering souvenirs, food and famous buttered bara brith, a loaf of bread similar to but lighter than fruitcake, although it reminded me of a fruit rock scone. The souvenir shop had some amazing art works and sculptures, which were unusual and unique. Although I would have loved to take some home, my suitcase was full and they were expensive.

Back on the coach again, we were headed to a ferry sailing at 2.40 pm to take us to Dublin. On our way, we drove through the majestic Snowdonia National Park. The views were spectacular, with nine mountain ranges and many peaks that were over 900 metres high. Driving through these mountain ranges was magical and I just loved their various landscapes of steep river gorges, waterfalls and green valleys.

Before heading to the ferry, we had our last rest stop at Llanfairpwllgwyngyll, a tongue twister for a name of a village. It had a huge restaurant and souvenir shop where we had lunch. I was looking for another vest and found a navy blue windcheater vest for €10, which I thought was reasonably priced.

Our next stop was the ferry, which was huge. Simon informed us on what to expect and made sure we had our passports ready just in case we were asked to show them. Steve drove the coach onto the ferry with precision and parked. Our next task was to ensure everyone went to the correct part of the ferry. We had to go up three flights of stairs into the blue section. This ferry was massive and had plenty of space to spread out. It also had a café and bar area where we could buy drinks and snacks. It also had a well-stocked souvenir shop with plenty of Irish paraphernalia. I was holding off on shopping until I arrived in Dublin as I was sure there would be plenty of shops there that I could buy heaps of souvenirs for the family.

Once settled, I wandered around and grabbed a coffee and bite to eat. We had at least three hours to kill, so as to entertain ourselves, we took photos with various members of the group posing with Cardboard Paul. I also had to transfer photos from my phone to my computer as my phone memory was full. Others in the group found a corner and decided to have a snooze.

The crossing was reasonably smooth without too many huge waves. I didn't feel seasick at all, which was fortunate. Once we were near our destination, we were instructed to meet in the blue area to make our way back down to the coach. Making sure none of us were left behind, Simon did a quick head count to ensure we were all on the coach. He also asked if anyone was missing and everyone shouted out that we were all there and accounted for, especially Cardboard Paul.

10
Ireland

Day 10 (cont.) – Arrival in Dublin

We were now on Irish soil and heading towards Dublin for our tour around the town prior to checking in to our hotel for the next few days, Clayton Hotel Leopardstown.

Dublin was huge and nothing like what I had expected, although I wasn't sure what to expect in the first place. After checking in to the hotel and bags of washing dropped off at reception, it was time to head out for our night at an Irish cabaret at Taylors Three Rock, a rambling farmhouse pub with the largest thatched roof in Ireland, soaring over 15 metres high. I was really looking forward to the evening, eating traditional Irish food, watching Irish dancing and singing along to the old Irish songs.

Sitting at very long tables, we were served a three-course meal. We started with fresh and delicious homemade cream vegetable soup, followed by our mains, which was a choice between, chicken, fish or lamb. I went for the traditional Irish lamb casserole – when in Ireland try the stews, as they say. Again, it was hearty and enjoyable. To top off the meal, we were served apple and cinnamon crunch with cream. With past experience attending floorshows, the meals can be disappointing. Fortunately, the meal was really tasty at this cabaret.

Once our meal was complete, the two-hour show began, with plenty of singing, Irish music, dancing and loads of laughter. The host for the night was Irish legend, Noel V Ginnity, who has long been recognised as Ireland's greatest comedian. He entertained the audience with his endless supply of funny stories, many based on Irish characters such as Mary and Paddy Murphy. We were in fits of laughter, and I had tears rolling down my face. In between our host's funny stories, the array of Irish dancing, music and singing was astounding.

Another main entertainer was male tenor, Rob Vickers, recognised as one of Ireland's greatest entertainer, singer, actor and musician.

He sang beautiful renditions of the Irish classics, like *Danny Boy* and *When You Were Sweet Sixteen*.

During the group Irish dancing, one of the dancers jumped from the stage and started to dance on our adjoining table – now that's what I call tabletop dancing. The dancer was extremely talented and cute. There was plenty of opportunity to take photos of the performers. Mary and Ben from our tour would photobomb me at every opportunity.

The evening had come to an end, and as we made our way out to our coach, it was confusing as there were more than one red Globus coach in the car park. We had to look out for our trusty guide Simon to point us in the right direction.

Day 11 – Dublin

Our day began with a hearty Irish breakfast in the dining room of our hotel with a guided half-day tour of Dublin in front of us.

We drove through the streets of Dublin with Simon pointing out major attractions and giving us a history lesson along the way. The architecture of old Dublin was beautiful and I was relieved to know that this city was proud of their buildings and kept them in good condition.

After our driving tour, Steve parked near Trinity College and Simon highlighted some places to explore and the time we were being picked up. As we meandered through the streets, I had kept a mental note of the areas I wanted to explore once we were dropped off.

Lisa, Marcie, Louise and I wandered up Kildare Street to the National Museum of Ireland, a beautiful building built in the 1850's which housed items as far back as the Viking Age. As we walked into the entrance of this grand building, the mosaic floor was magnificent, detailed and intricate with many different patterns and designs on the floor.

10. Ireland

The change in energy could be felt by both Louise and I as we walked through the different displays. I was fascinated with the Celtic and medieval art, viewing the Ardagh Chalice, Tara Brooch and Derrynaflan Hoard. My main interest was the Kingship and Sacrifice exhibition where it showed the discovery of two Iron Age bog bodies at Oldcroghan in County Offaly and Clonycavan in County Meath. The remains were found in a bog dating between 400 BC and 200 BC and were in a remarkably good state of preservation. When I had a closer look at these bodies, I could definitely feel a change in the air and energy, and it gave me tingles. The detail of fingers belonging to 'Oldcroghan Man' were that of an old man, real, life-like and amazing.

As we wandered around the museum, I was feeling the energy shift from one part to another and could hear children laughing and running, although there were no children around. The energy became very heavy and dense as we walked upstairs to another exhibition.

We had been at the museum for a while but there were still so much more to discover, so we walked back down Kildare Street towards Trinity College. Lisa and Marcie had already been through the college and decided to split up. We agreed to meet up later. Louise and I walked through a cobblestone courtyard past the expansive gardens and the Book of Kells Exhibition. We decided not to queue up with the other tourists, instead we walked through the courtyard and explored the grounds of the college.

The day was beautiful and warm as we wandered through the courtyard, picking up the different old energies as we made our way through the old buildings. I was certainly becoming more in tuned with the different energies of all these old cities, and picking up old souls along the way.

We made our way out of Trinity College, wanting to head towards the Viking exhibition I had seen earlier. With map in hand, we were making a good effort of not getting lost, but to no avail. All the streets seemed to be the same and we were walking in circles. After a while we stood on a major intersection and ended up asking someone for directions. We were completely lost and heading in the total opposite direction to where we wanted to be. Once back on the right road, we wandered towards the Viking exhibition, passing pubs, cafés and many clothing shops, past the Molly Malone statue, and walking into the odd shop having a look at all the different fashions of clothes and shoes.

We arrived at our destination and paid our tickets for the Viking & Medieval Dublin Experience at Dublinia Viking Museum, and declined on paying an extra €7 just to walk through the Christ Church Cathedral. I had already been in too many churches and they all seemed to look the same. The statue of the Viking that greeted us at the doorway reminded me of our tour guide Simon, the resemblance was uncanny.

This exhibition was very informative and interesting and took us back to the days of the Vikings. The displays were life-like and they made it seem as if we were there back in time. The exhibition was also interactive as you could try on Viking clothes, although Louise and I declined and continued strolling down a noisy street and visited a smoky and cramped Viking house. The exhibition was on multiple levels and we made our way up each level, then through the back of the cathedral, and out into the sunshine and fresh air.

We headed back to where the bus had dropped us off. Along the way we bumped into Lisa and Marcia, who were heading up towards St Patrick's Cathedral and asked if we wanted to tag along. Again, I declined as I was trying not to visit too many churches for various reasons.

On our way back, we were looking for somewhere to eat as we hadn't had lunch yet and were starting to feel hungry. All the cafés and pubs we passed by were either busy, cramped or just not quite what we were looking for.

We found Trinity College again and knew we were in the right place. Wandering down Nassau Street, we walked past the Knobs and Knockers shop that was painted in bright blue and sold door knobs and knockers – believe it or not. Around the corner behind the shop was the Brewbaker Café where we found a table and ordered a sandwich and coffee. After lunch we had about an hour to kill before being collected. We found a large souvenir shop where I purchased an Irish fridge magnet for Pauline, a polo shirt for Matthew and an Irish plastic duck for Ollie.

Once back at the hotel, it was a quick change of clothes before heading downstairs to the lounge bar for a quick drink prior to heading out for the night for a tour of the Guinness Storehouse and private dinner at its restaurant.

The Guinness Storehouse, located at St. James's Gate Brewery, was busy with many other tourists and we were fortunate to have our own private tour. The Storehouse covered seven floors, surrounding a glass atrium shaped in the form of a pint of Guinness. The ground floor introduced the beer's four ingredients and the brewery's founder, Arthur Guinness. Other exhibits featured the history of Guinness advertising, and even included an interactive exhibit on responsible drinking.

The seventh floor housed the Gravity Bar with views of Dublin and was packed with other visitors wanting their pint of Guinness that was included in the admission price. Unfortunately, the views of Dublin were obstructed due to dark clouds and rain.

After our tour, we were escorted into the large restaurant that was empty except for the twenty of us that were on the tour. Vegetable soup was on the menu again, it tended to be a standard entrée at all of our meals.

Our tour guide gave us an introduction of how to drink Guinness. It was all in the technique, breathing through your nose first before taking a swig. I was not a fan of Guinness prior to this evening, but after the demonstration, I decided to try a drop and fell in love with the taste, to the point now that I prefer it over other beers. Everyone raised their glasses and said to each other *sláinte*, pronounced 'slawn-che', meaning health.

After filling ourselves with food and Guinness, it was time to head back to the hotel for an early night as we would be back on the road the next morning. Before heading up to my room, I collected my clean laundry so I could pack them into my suitcase.

Day 12 – Dublin – Kildare – Cashel – Limerick

Back on the road, our tour family were back together and discussing our past two days in Dublin and showing what was bought, for all those shopaholics. Mary and Ben had to buy another suitcase each to pack all the souvenirs they had purchased for their families.

As we rolled out of Dublin, I realised that the answers and clarity that I was seeking from my spiritual guides were not forthcoming. I sat quietly and meditated for a few moments asking why I had not received any answers but I received no reply. No doubt I had to wait and see what was coming up. I knew that by the time my *#tripofalifetime* had ended, I would have the answers I was seeking. It was always about timing. I couldn't rush these things and had to immerse myself into the experience and just enjoy myself and have fun, which was what I was definitely doing.

As much as I enjoyed myself in Dublin, the city itself didn't give me that connection that I was seeking. Unlike some other cities I had visited over the past few weeks, I didn't feel as though I wanted to come back and visit this city again. I am sure if I had spent a longer time in the city and explored more, my experience would have been different.

Cardboard Paul was safe and seated in his own row as we headed towards Kildare. The country side was green and lush as I had expected in Ireland.

Our first stop for the day was the Irish National Stud at Kildare where horses were bred on the 800 acre site since 1900. Colonel William Hall Walker had a passion for racehorses and set about turning the Tully land in Kildare into one of Europe's premier studs. He succeeded, even if some of his ideas and beliefs were not the norm.

10. Ireland

We gathered at the statue of Hall Walker where our guide commenced our forty minutes tour around this expansive property. We walked through the stud where different statues with astrological theme could be seen. There were horses everywhere, from miniature horses that were very adorable to wooden carvings of horses that looked real from a distance. We walked through the magnificent St. Fiachra's Garden, which was completely natural and had beautiful lakes and a statue of the man himself, known for his charitable work and devotion to those in need of help.

The astrologically inclined Colonel not only loved horses but also horticulture. Under his direction, the magnificent Japanese Gardens were created. The gardens were created by Tassa Eida between 1906 and 1910, telling a story of life through rocks, trees, water and more. My favourite sign in the gardens was the one that showed 'Path of Life' to the left and 'Easy Path' to the right. I certainly knew which path I was on and it wasn't too easy.

After our walk through the gardens we went to explore the Japanese Gardens restaurant for some morning tea. As I was paying for my tea and lemon tart, the cashier asked where I was from. I answered Melbourne, Australia, and she told me that she had just returned from Colac, Victoria. I asked if she happened to know a friend of mine called Michael – and she did. I said to her, 'It's such a small world.'

We were back on the road again, weaving through the Irish landscape heading towards Cashel, our next stop for lunch. The advantage of having a tour guide was that they tend to know the best places to eat in each of the small towns. Our next stop was a small café with delicious food that didn't disappoint. Those that wanted to hike up the hill to visit another church ruin took the opportunity to visit St Mary's Cathedral, King John's castle and the rock of Cashel. Louise and I decided to walk along the quaint streets of the village instead.

On our way to Limerick, we drove through the town Tipperary, and of course, what would you expect to be played but the song *It's a Long Way to Tipperary*. We arrived in our accommodation for the evening, the Absolute Hotel Limerick. Steve had to reverse the bus up a steep incline to park in front of the hotel, which was a bit scary considering the streets were very narrow.

Our entertainment for the evening was at the Knappogue Castle Medieval Banquet. Stepping back in time, we were greeted at the door by the Earl's butler and the ladies of the castle offering goblets of honey mead. Whilst standing around drinking our mead and waiting to be seated, the hosts asked Simon to choose the King and Queen for the evening. The honour went to our fellow Aussie husband and wife, Julie and Ray, from Bathurst. We were escorted to our table by the gorgeous ladies in full medieval dress and when everyone was seated, the King and Queen were introduced to a roar of shouts and claps. They were seated at the head table with other guests that were nominated for various other roles of the evening.

I was attempting to sit on the bench when Lisa asked if I wanted help to 'get my leg over'. I absolutely lost it with laughter. Lisa was looking at me funny and after I composed myself, I whispered in her ear what it meant. She gave me a stunned look and then started laughing. It must be an Aussie thing; our humour must seem very weird to others. I hadn't laughed that much in such a long time. It was really refreshing to laugh and let my hair down, and just relax and enjoy the moment. I was having so much fun, the experience was amazing.

The meal comprised of a choice of smoked salmon or tomato basil soup for entrée, supreme chicken with creamed potatoes and roasted vegetables for mains, and apple and cinnamon crunch for dessert, not forgetting plenty of red and white wine to go around. The meal was delicious and one of the best cabaret meals I had tasted on my whole tour to date. It was another evening of amazing singing and Irish dancing with some very talented entertainers.

Our group had a few drinks by the time we were back on the bus and there was much singing and merriment as we drove back to our hotel. After we arrived, a few of us decided to have a night cap. We were sitting around and Steve came and sat with us. Gail and Hans were there as well, and I think Gail had a few too many meads as she reminded me of a naughty school girl. Gail kept telling us that the mead had drugs in it and everyone just laughed. She had this infectious laugh and was hilarious to watch.

Hans and Lisa started to interrogate Steve, wanting to know more about who he was. Steve was from Wales, on his second marriage and had four kids. He told us that this was his first tour with Simon and I was surprised considering that they just clicked and worked really well together.

I was chatting to Gail about Paul and she told me that she had lost her brother to diabetes and sister-in-law to lung cancer. Gail thought I was brave and amazing for keeping my promise to Paul and travelling with him as a cardboard cut-out. She admired me.

Each one of us have our stories and carry our battle scars, their effect on you depend on how you react to them.

Day 13 – Limerick – West Coast Excursion

We were staying in Limerick another day and headed out to explore the west coast. There was news coming in that a hurricane was building out at sea on the coast of Ireland and was heading landwards in the next few days.

Simon was very casual and blasé about the situation and kept telling us that this was normal, the storm heading towards us was a usual Irish storm and would blow over before hitting land. Our American friends didn't see it that way and were very concerned, considering the damage caused by Hurricane Irma in Florida and Harvey in Houston.

So far, I had been missing all the hurricanes in the USA, whether they were ahead of me or came after me just when I left the area. I wasn't really prepared to be hit by a hurricane directly. It was a very nervous few days as we waited for the news to confirm when it was actually hitting the coast of Ireland.

We were heading for the Cliffs of Moher and I was really looking forward to this. The weather was overcast and drizzly, which I expected was the beginnings of the wild weather just about to hit us. The Cliffs of Moher were spectacular, although the wind was cutting right through us. I decided to leave Cardboard Paul on the coach as I didn't want him to get wet – or worse, blow off from the cliffs.

A group of us wandered up to the top of the cliffs and stared in awe of the majestic cliffs with the sea crashing against them. It was an amazing sight to see. We climbed up to O'Brien's Tower to get a better view, as well as to protect ourselves from the biting wind. After contending with the wind, we walked back down the hill into the visitor's centre to walk around and a have quick wander into the gift shop to see what they had for sale.

The news on Hurricane Ophelia was ramping up, with the storm regarded as the worst storm to affect Ireland in fifty years, and was also the easternmost major hurricane in the Atlantic on record.

Our next stop was the port city of Galway. We were dropped off at the Latin Quarter which extended from the Spanish Arch to O'Brien's Bridge to St Nicholas' Church to Middle Street and featured many fine examples of the city's medieval heritage. We wandered down a short stretch of cobblestone road, known as High Street, past many shops looking for somewhere to eat. We found a restaurant where I sat down to a scrumptious Irish shepherd's pie. On our way back to the bus, we came across a father and his young sons busking, playing music for the crowd and collecting a dollar or two.

Our next stop was Rathbaun Farm. As we arrived and alighted the bus, we were greeted by farmer Fintan Connolly who guided us through to the sheds. He introduced us to all the different breeds of sheep and gave a short lecture about sheep farming. We then walked through a small paddock for a sheepdog demonstration. Watching the extremely smart and quick sheepdog herding the sheep was very entertaining.

After the sheepherding demonstrations, we returned to the main building to freshen up and sit for tea, coffee and scones fresh out of the oven. The tea room was attached to the 250 year old house where the owner was raised. It was restored to its 18th century condition and was lovely, with a peat fire in the large open hearth. The scones were yummy and topped off nicely with jam and fresh cream.

We were back on the road towards our hotel before our big night out again. The days and nights were becoming tiring and taking its toll on many of our tour family, with Simon being hit worst by a cold virus going around the bus. Fortunately, I hadn't been affected yet and was still taking my vitamins to keep it at bay.

Later that night, Simon informed us that Hurricane Ophelia was serious, and that Globus had put in place contingency plans to ensure our safety. Plan B was to leave Limerick early in the morning to beat the storm and be off the roads. Our tour of the Ring of Kerry was cancelled. Although disappointing, safety was our priority. We would be headed to Killarney early in the morning to stay ahead of the hurricane.

Our final night in Limerick was spent at the Bunratty Castle & Folk Park. It was a magical night of Irish music, dance, song, stories and traditional food. We were escorted to our tables and I had a seat front and centre of the stage. The entertainment was great, but unfortunately, the food was very disappointing, average and certainly not worth £69.

We were entertained by a group of talented singers and dancers. One of the Irish dancers was performing a so-called broom dance, dancing around a broom whilst leaping to the beat of the music. He was extremely talented and an amazing dancer. After a few songs and dances, we had a group sing-along to *The Wild Rover*, which was a favourite Irish song of mine. It brought back many happy memories of when I was a child visiting my Irish uncle and his family. Hence, I knew the words fairly well and was singing away with gusto.

After the song, the host – who reminded me very much of my brother-in-law – called me up on stage to perform the broom dance. Now I had learnt some Irish dancing when I was in my teens, but I was not the fittest person and age was not on my side. After a quick chat and few laughs, the music started, I grabbed the broom and started prancing around the stage, sweeping it and keeping up with the music. The music kept going and I was becoming puffed out from all the dancing and running around the stage. We had been going for a few minutes when I finally ran out of puff.

Before I stopped, I did a quick Irish jig and then gave up. I walked back down – or rather, staggered back down – to my seat after I was given a round of applause and a gift of an Irish book and CD. I was fortunate to have Louise record the footage of my big performance. It was something I will always remember with fondness.

News of my stage performance quickly spread around the group. Simon said that they must have liked me as they usually pull people off the stage within a few minutes and I was dancing on stage for at least five minutes before giving up. I had a *craic* of a time being the stage ham.

Day 14 – Limerick – Killarney

News reports were coming in that all the schools were closed and transport cancelled – it was red alert all over Ireland.

We were up and on the road early in the hopes of outrunning the hurricane that was hitting us later that morning. The government was taking it extremely serious and advising all its citizens in the area to remain indoors. The bus ride was fairly subdued with majority of us feeling tired and half of us feeling sick with whatever bug was going around. Plus, I think most of us were quietly worried about how this hurricane was going to affect us, and if we were going to be stuck in Killarney. Simon had been in contact with the hotel and they were aware of the situation.

We arrived at Killarney Towers Hotel and it was packed with other tour groups waiting out the storm. As we arrived earlier than planned, and other groups couldn't leave, the hotel staff were extremely busy trying to rearrange rooms and organise food.

10. Ireland

Our group found a corner of the lounge and sat waiting for a few hours until we were given our rooms. The bar was open, and there was a Starbucks available as well. All our American travellers in the group thought it was great and started ordering coffees all around. The hotel had offered us an Irish coffee and hot chocolate. I tried the Irish coffee but found the cream on top disgusting, though once I stirred it in, the coffee was warm and filling.

Another huge tour group from the USA had started singing *The Star-Spangled Banner*. Some of us non-Americans found this rather insulting considering we were in Ireland. I was not sure why they decided to sing the American national anthem and I was not the only one that looked puzzled. They then continued to sing a variety of songs to keep themselves entertained whilst sitting out the storm.

The lounge area was filling up fast with families and couples looking for something to eat. After a few hours, we ordered lunch and another Starbucks coffee. Unfortunately, due to the amount of people, we had to wait but we could understand the hotel's dilemma. The staff were really friendly and helpful. Steve and Simon sat at the bar and drank whisky whilst waiting for their rooms.

Some brave souls ventured out into the weather and went shopping, although I don't think there was much open. You could hear the wind slamming against the windows and doors. Although I didn't want to venture out into the elements, I had to go next door for cash before the ATM machines were blown away by the force of the wind.

What was it with me and these hurricanes? I had, to different extents, encountered Harvey hitting Houston, Maria hitting New York, and now Ophelia.

We were finally given our room keys and access to our rooms. Lisa and I had made arrangements to meet in the hotel's indoor swimming pool in a few hours for a swim.

I entered my hotel room and unpacked Cardboard Paul. I was not going to let this opportunity pass me by with the hurricane bellowing outside. I grabbed Cardboard Paul and put a shower cap on his head and took some photos. I also had his rain poncho ready to go. This photo is one of my favourite photos of us together and sits proudly on the front cover of this book.

I was extremely tired as the touring was taking its toll on me. I was tossing up whether to go for a swim or climb into bed and have a nanna nap. I decided to unpack my bathers and head to the pool for a swim. Part of the hotel's swimming rules was that you had to wear a bathing cap. I didn't have one with me, so I bought one of their unflattering blue bathing caps, not thinking that I could have used the clear plastic shower cap that was sitting on Cardboard Paul's head.

The swimming pool was huge and had a spa pool on the side. It was fairly quiet with only a few of us using the facilities. I sat in the spa for about an hour before a group of men decided to join me. I then swam over to the pool section and did a few laps in the Olympic-size pool. The pool looked very Roman, and I pictured the Roman days with women gathering around chatting whilst lazing in the water. The water was warm and very relaxing. After a few hours, I decided to head back to my room for a shower and a lie down for a quick nanna nap. I wasn't quite sure where Lisa was as she hadn't appeared – probably having a nanna nap as well.

Day 15 – Killarney – Blarney – Waterford

The news of the hurricane was coming in with reports involving heavy damages and three people dead. A woman and a man died in separate incidents when trees fell on their cars. Another man died in a chainsaw accident while attempting to remove a tree felled by the storm. I couldn't understand why people were out in the storm, considering that everyone was advised not to venture outside.

Many people were stuck because of the lethal winds and stormy rains. Thousands of businesses and homes in North Ireland and Wales, along with 360,000 people in the Republic of Ireland, suffered from a power outage. With a speed of 190 kilometres per hour, Ophelia generated waves of over 60 metres before it made landfall and wreaked havoc in the region. The roofs of houses and schools flew off with the winds, trampolines were seen rolling through the lanes, roads jammed by fallen trees and many such incidents were reported. The skies in most of the area turned red and bright yellow as Ophelia dragged the dust with the winds from the Sahara.

We survived Hurricane Ophelia, and as we headed towards our next destination, Waterford, you could see the damage that Ophelia caused with the trees uprooted and branches on roads. The feeling was really eerie as we cruised through the towns.

One of the highlights for the day was the visit to Blarney Castle. Mary and Ben were getting very excited as this visit was on their bucket list, they had planned to kiss the Blarney Stone. Kissing Ireland's Blarney Stone was a tradition that's been around for several centuries, said to give a person the gift of eloquence and persuasiveness. I wasn't particularly interested in lying on my back, leaning backwards while holding onto two railings and being held by a stranger to kiss an old stone that others had been kissing. Also, I think I had enough eloquence and persuasiveness that I didn't need any more.

Unfortunately, when we arrived at the Blarney Castle, it was closed due to the damages within the grounds during Hurricane Ophelia, with trees uprooted and blown over. Louise and I went for a walk towards Blarney Castle and peered over the wall. All you could see were branches and fallen trees everywhere. I took the opportunity to take Cardboard Paul out and take some photos from the car park in front of Blarney Castle.

After our walk, we headed back towards the Blarney Woollen Mills Irish heritage shop and café for a look around and something to eat. There were tourists everywhere and the place was very busy. The heritage shop itself was massive and had plenty of Irish woollen clothes for sale that was expensive and well out of my budget.

We had arrived in Waterford and was greeted by our guide, Jack, on a private walking tour of this gorgeous city. Our first stop was lunch in a café highly recommended by Simon. The food was delicious and had a welcoming feeling to sit in and have a good cup of tea. Our next stop was next door in the gift shop to pick up any last minute souvenirs. Lisa and Marcie were looking at the Celtic jewellery and I spotted a lovely necklace and matching earrings in silver and gold. I also found another necklace perfect for my soul sister, Gail, for her birthday. There were a few in the group – not mentioning names, but they will know who they are – that went crazy buying up various gifts. The undercarriage of the coach was packed to the brim with all the extra suitcase being purchased along the way.

Our next stop was Reginald's Tower, an impressive and tall historic tower built with brick and had a model Viking long boat standing next to it.

Jack, who was known for his master storytelling, didn't disappoint and lived up to his reputation. He proceeded to tell our group the history of the Vikings that founded Waterford City some 1,100 years ago and the extensive trading links with Viking settlements overseas. He then led us through to the back of the tower, which stood the ruins of Greyfriars Church. Jack continued to tell us the history of the Vikings and the Normans, including the story of Strongbow.

By this time, we had come to an open area where Jack called upon some volunteers from our group to play the characters in the marriage ceremony between Strongbow and Aoife, daughter of the King of Leinster. It was very funny and entertaining especially for those that went into character.

Our next stop was the Christchurch Cathedral, designed by John Roberts. The cathedral had been on the monumental site since 1096, and it was here that Strongbow married Aoife in 1170. This was, therefore, one of the most important historic sites in Ireland. There, I lit two candles, one for Paul and one for Mum.

It was time to say farewell to Jack as he dropped us off at the House of Waterford Crystal for our tour through the factory and to see how crystal was made. Some of us were very nervous walking through the factory, and especially past some of the crystal pieces. On the first part of the tour, we were given the opportunity to hold some crystal pieces. I didn't want any part of it, but Ben and Gerard were happy to hold a crystal gridiron football. Everyone was holding their breaths, hoping they wouldn't drop it.

We were taken through the entire process of crystal making and then brought to the showroom with all the beautiful Waterford crystals on display and for sale. I looked at a few pieces and kept walking, as I wasn't in the market to purchase anything so exquisite, let alone afford it.

We had some spare time whilst waiting to be picked up, so we wandered into the Waterford Crystal coffee shop for some cake and coffee.

It was our last night in Ireland, and what better way to send us off from Ireland than by having our own private concert with Irish recording artist, Richie Roberts, singing Irish folk songs, and drinking Guinness in the Aggie Hayes Pub.

On our way to Aggie Hayes Pub, we picked up Richie and headed to the harbour in Dunmore East to see the Celtic Sea while driving past many traditional Irish houses. As we arrived a day after Ophelia hit, the sea was very rough and fallen trees could be seen. After a few photographs for the group, we were back on the coach travelling towards the pub.

Aggie Hayes Pub was a bright yellow, thatched roof pub that has been owned and ran by the same family for over 300 years. It was one of Ireland's best kept secrets, perched on the cliff edge in the south eastern shores of the Celtic Sea. We were very privileged to have our own private party at this quaint and very old pub.

We lined up and ordered our drinks – I ordered a Guinness, of course – and then we headed into the lounge area where Richie was already setting up to sing. Sitting in the tight space and the chatter of the group getting louder, the music started, and we were singing along with Richie at the top of our voices. A few of the couples were up and dancing. Our few hours were up, and as we headed back to the bus, a few of us, myself included, purchased Richie's CD of Irish songs.

On the way back to our hotel it was dark and raining with Irish music blaring. We were all singing and laughing far too much, we even had an appearance of the dancing neck pillows that were left on the bus, it topped off one of the best nights on our tour.

Once back at the hotel, we had our final dinner in Ireland. As we sat around and chatted, we realised that we were heading back tomorrow to Wales, with only four days left before we arrived back in London to leave our little tour family.

We were up early to board the coach for our ferry crossing from Rosslare to Pembroke and back to British soil. The ferry back was rather relaxing with everyone spreading out, some getting a bite to eat and others exploring the souvenir shop to buy those last Irish gifts for family and friends back home. I unpacked Cardboard Paul and sat him on one of the chairs. Louise took some photos whilst others in the group gathered around and had a photo opportunity with Cardboard Paul as well.

We had the odd look from other passengers on board, which I found amusing. What other cardboard cut-out can say they have travelled on the ferry from Ireland to Britain?

Day 16 – Waterford – Cardiff

We were in Wales, and of course, the music was changed to Welsh, with the anthem of Wales and choral music playing on the bus. We didn't have to wait long before the music of the famous Welshman himself, Tom Jones, came on with *It's Not Unusual*. Lisa and I started chair dancing again and the neck pillows made a comeback.

We arrived in Cardiff, the capital of Wales and its largest city. It was Wales's chief commercial centre and the base for most national cultural institutions and Welsh media. Our entertainment for the evening was a Welsh experience with dinner at the Wales Millennium Centre, situated at the heart of Cardiff Bay. This building was impressive, modern and spacious.

The entertainment was a group from the talented national opera singers and musicians who performed Welsh music, both in English and Welsh, and even had a harp player. The Master of Ceremony for the evening promised that there was going to be a performance from their famous Welshman, Tom Jones. Everyone knew that he was lying, but Lisa and I were quietly hoping that he would make an appearance.

Day 17 – Cardiff – Bath – Glastonbury – Dartmoor - Exeter

We were heading towards Exeter via Bath today for the last few days of our tour. I didn't know what to expect from Bath and was pleasantly surprised by this beautiful old town. Bath was a World Heritage site located in the South West of England, known primarily for its Roman and Georgian heritage.

We had a tour booked for the Roman Baths and had a quick tour around town. Unfortunately, it was raining heavily outside, so visibility out the windows was poor. We drove past the Jane Austen Centre and this piqued my interest, as Jane Austen was my favourite author. I was hoping that I had enough time to have a look around the centre.

The Roman Baths was constructed around 70 AD as a grand bathing and socialising complex, it was one of the best-preserved Roman remains in the world, where 1,170,000 litres of steaming spring water, reaching 46°C, still fills the bathing site every single day. The Roman Baths was the site of extensive ruins and an interactive museum filled with many treasures and visual snippets that transported you back to Roman times and the lives of the Aquae Sulis people.

We lined up and handed over our tickets and were given the audio player that we plugged Globus headphones into. We walked on the ancient pavements as the Romans did two thousand years ago, and explored ancient chambers which historically housed changing rooms and tepid plunge pools.

Louise and I walked through the baths and found it extremely busy with other tourists and schoolchildren. As we entered into the depths of the baths, spooky things started to happen. The energy changed and became cold. I shivered and said to Louise, 'This will be fun, and can you feel that?' She agreed with me.

As we walked further towards the Roman Baths, Louise was struck on the face by some unknown spirit and immediately felt the pain in her right cheek. I, on the other hand, had feelings of enclosure and entrapment. As I continued to walk towards the main baths, I was letting any spirits know that if they wanted to move on, we could meet at the baths in the centre of the building.

When I arrived, I could feel this heaviness and I sat quietly and meditated and asked for all the spirits to bring their guides in close. I could see in my mind's eye that a huge portal had opened up in the middle of the baths and that a vortex was in action, taking all those that had been stuck in that place for centuries. The portal was opened for approximately five minutes and then closed. For all those spirits that needed to move on, they did.

Once I opened my eyes again I could feel the shift in energy and it was much lighter. I had a quick chat with Louise and told her what I experienced, and she confirmed that the energy was so much better and lighter than when we first arrived. The experience was amazing and fulfilling, as I was following my purpose of helping others, whether it be humans or spiritual beings. In all my years of working with spirits, I have never experienced a portal opening up, let alone seeing it and watching the vortex take those souls that had been stuck for thousands of years. It was surreal.

Once the energy was lighter, I took an opportunity to take some photos around the large bath that looked like an Olympic swimming pool. As it was raining heavily, I had left Cardboard Paul on the coach, not wanting to get him wet.

It was still raining heavily as we came out of the baths. We were hungry so we started looking for something to eat. As we walked through the cobblestone streets, we came across a very fancy upmarket restaurant that seemed to be the only decent place in the area that offered shelter from the pouring rain and wasn't crowded. We ordered some hot vegetable soup each and a bowl of fries to share.

Opposite the restaurant was a shop that sold homemade fudge. As a huge lover of fudge, I walked in and I was overcome by this wonderful, sweet perfume in the air. There were cabinets full of different coloured and flavoured fudge. I felt like I was in Willy Wonka's chocolate factory. I had to make the difficult decision of which flavour to buy out of all the different types of fudge on display. I went a bit crazy and bought a few different blocks of sea salted caramel, Belgium chocolate swirl, Mocha Coca swirl and lemon meringue fudge. It was so delicious, sweet, smooth and gooey – not very good for the teeth or the waist line.

We walked along the narrow laneways and found a post office for Louise to send some mail back home. Whilst walking around the post office, I found a notebook that had the entire story of *Pride and Prejudice* printed in tiny font that serves as page lines in the notebook. I purchased the book and treasured the uniqueness of it.

Unfortunately, our time in Bath had come to an end and I was sad that I didn't get the opportunity to visit the Jane Austen Centre. I made a mental note to put it on my list for my next visit to this beautiful part of the world.

It was dark as we meandered through the hills and narrow laneways, with rain persistent outside. We were headed to our dinner at the local pub in The Old Inn, located at Widecombe in the Moor, Dartmoor. The coach parked near the Church of St Pancras and we walked through the churchyard. It was extremely impressive and beautiful, with a 36-metre spire which earned it the title of 'Cathedral of the Moors'. The church was built in the late gothic perpendicular style, dated from the 14th century. You could feel the eeriness in the air as we walked past the church. I was getting shivers, but I was not sure if it was the coldness and rain or because the church area was haunted. I was certainly picking up on the energy.

We were escorted to our tables and had the warmth coming from the open fires strategically placed around the large restaurant. I ordered my drink of choice – Guinness, of course – and had a hearty meal of vegetable soup, chicken breast topped with slow roast BBQ pulled pork and melted cheddar served with chips, dressed leaves and slaw – it was delicious.

After our meal, we headed towards the bus in the dark and through the haunted churchyard again. It felt very eerie and I was sure I saw something dark move from the corner of my eye. A headless horseman, maybe? I think I had watched too many of my favourite episodes of *Midsummer Murders*.

We had arrived at the Mecure Exeter Hotel and I had a message from Ken, who I had arranged to meet up with him and his wife Marja whilst I was calling through Exeter. He had been trying to contact me on my mobile but I was in and out of range, so we missed each other. Also, he didn't leave his contact number for me to call him back. After dinner and back in my room, Ken finally rang and after a quick chat, we arranged to meet in town the next day. He said he would call to confirm the time in the morning.

Day 18 – Exeter

Our hotel in Exeter was modern and had amazing quirky art on the wall. The painting next to my room was based on the famous painting *Girl with the Pearl Earring*, but the girl was also wearing swimming goggles and a swimming cap.

The last day of my tour was quiet. The tour group went to Plymouth Sound for a boat tour, whereas I caught up with Marja and Ken, old friends from Australasian Fleet Management Association (AfMA) back in Melbourne. We had arranged to meet in town somewhere and they were going to give me a call with directions.

10. Ireland

It was a nice feeling to take my time, casually having some breakfast and not having to rush anywhere. When joining a tour like this, it is really good to have some alone, quiet time. Although I had a room to myself, at night I would usually be preparing my case for the next day, catching up with family, updating Facebook and then sleeping. I was always on the go doing something or getting ready. You can't necessarily rest or relax on the coach as there was always something to see. Most of the time, Simon would be giving us historical information, music would be playing and the other tour buddies would be chatting.

I wandered around the quaint town and headed to the local shopping centre, Guildhall. I walked past the magnificent Gothic architecture of the Cathedral Church of St Peter, and through spacious gardens where the locals mingled and sat on the grass soaking up the sun on this reasonably warm day – it was picturesque. There were all the major stores as I walked through the shopping centre, but I didn't buy anything significant, only snacks for the next day on the road.

I found a coffee shop behind Guildhall and ordered a coffee and chocolate muffin as I did not have enough breakfast and was already feeling hungry.

Marja and Ken arranged to meet at a local patisserie at 11.30 am. I arrived a little earlier and stood out the front waiting and looking for their familiar faces. I didn't have to wait too long as I saw them both swaggering down the street towards me. We greeted each other warmly with big hugs and kisses. I was really glad to see these familiar faces. We went inside and sat down in a booth and ordered something scrumptious.

I have known Marja and Ken for over eleven years from our association with AfMA where I was on the board. It was good to see that they were both well and really enjoying their life back home.

I gave Marja my last copy of *Conversations with Paul* that I had on this tour. Marja and Ken both knew all about Paul and were in Melbourne when he was sick. They even met him a few times at the different functions we attended together for AfMA. It was lovely catching up with them both and seeing friendly faces from home. I gave them both a big hug and wished them well and walked back to the hotel.

It was officially the last night on the road. The tour group sat to dinner in the hotel restaurant, chatting and sharing our thoughts and experiences of the day. I was starting to get tired, with the constant travelling, early mornings and late nights – they were starting to take their toll on me. The continuous change of hotels and beds were causing my back to stiffen and ache, I desperately needed a massage.

I was also surrounded by some negative people that was draining my energy. Unfortunately, we had a few on this tour, but I was having too much fun and surrounded myself with positive people to not let them bother me.

Day 19 – Exeter – Stonehenge – London

I was really excited and looking forward to my visit to Stonehenge as I knew that by the time I had left there, I would have clarity of my direction and where I was going.

A couple on our tour decided to tell anyone who would listen that they had already been there, and in their opinion, it was nothing to look at and was very disappointing. Stonehenge was on top of my list of places I wanted to visit so I was not impressed when I heard their comment. I thought it best if you had a negative opinion about a certain place, you keep it to yourself. It was like seeing a movie and then telling others who haven't seen it the plot, the whole story and the ending. Why spoil it for others?

For me, visiting Stonehenge was a spiritual journey, and the energy was building even before I arrived at this sacred place. No words could describe this awesome experience.

I had seen a beautiful rainbow as we approached Stonehenge and knew that this was going to be extremely special. I was going to get the answers I was seeking from my spirit guides. All was going to unfold here at this sacred site.

10. Ireland

Louise and I stepped off the coach, and arm in arm we walked up towards the bus that would take us to the stones. I had Cardboard Paul tucked safely into his calico bag across my left shoulder. As soon as I stepped onto the pathway, I was crying – absolutely sobbing – and I couldn't stop. I couldn't explain the emotion that overcame me.

Louise and I just couldn't put into words what we were experiencing but we came up with the feeling of nothingness. It described exactly what the energy was about; it was silent, so quiet, so peaceful and tranquil, as if time stood still and we had walked into another dimension. It was an amazing and life-changing experience.

By the time we stepped onto the bus that would take us up to the stones, we had composed ourselves. We stood there with the others, holding on to our high expectations – when we arrived at the stones, we were not disappointed. The energy in this place was surreal and quiet. Although there were crowds around us, and the wind and rain were coming in sideways, we were in a totally different time and space. I had the feeling of coming home and felt sad but also happy. My heart was full with gratitude that I was able to come home again and knew that I had walked here thousands of years ago as a druid. The flashbacks started, and I could see my fellow druids gathering around the fire.

We walked further around the stones trying to find a place that wasn't too windy or crowded so I could take Cardboard Paul out for a photo opportunity. We found a less windy place to take a few photos of Cardboard Paul and me standing in front of the Stonehenge, although people were everywhere and getting in our way. I had to hold onto him super tight as the wind was so strong and the sleet rain was coming in sideways. I was concerned that he would fly off.

My spidey senses were tingling as we continued to walk around the stones and imagining back when the druids walked this part of the earth. I had a strong sense of belonging and being back home.

We walked back to the bus that would take us back to the Stonehenge Visitor Centre so we could explore more, read up on the history and grab something to eat.

In front of the centre were numerous huts and large stones on display. As I was walking out of one of the huts, I had the answers that I was seeking. My spirit guides told me that the answers are within me. *Look into your heart for the answers.* There was no use looking outside or to others for the answers as they were within me. The answers to my questions will always remain in my heart. The answers would come when I tapped into my heart source. I shook my head, how simple was this message?

I finally had direction and the answers I had been seeking since Paris.

My visit to the Stonehenge was life-changing and I couldn't describe the experience, it was breathtaking and amazing – it was nothingness.

As we made our way back to London, another beautiful rainbow appeared in the distance not far from where the Stonehenge stood. It was magical.

We had arrived at our hotel for the last night, the Park Plaza Westminster Bridge London. Our luggage was piled up on the pathway, and before I grabbed my suitcase and overnight bag, I gave Steve and Simon a big hug and thanked them for the tour. Some other tour buddies gave envelopes of gratuity, mine was already included as part of the tour package.

Luggage in hand and Cardboard Paul safely tucked under my arm, I lined up at the reception desk for my room key. As this was our last time together, we bid our farewells and hugged each other as we went on our separate ways. Some of us had booked into different dinners and shows and some stayed in-house to relax and unwind. I was sad to say goodbye to the tour family. Promises of keeping in touch were given, phone numbers and Facebook details were exchanged.

I went up to my room and placed my case on the bed and started to sort out what I was going to wear for my night out. I booked the *Dreamgirls* dinner and show on the West End and was being picked up by another tour group.

10. Ireland

I was sitting quietly on the bed and I suddenly had this horrific pain creep up on me on the left-hand side of my stomach. I only had a small quantity of Panadol on me, so I took two of them hoping that the pain would subside. I had no idea what it was and the pain persisted.

I went down to the lobby to meet the other guests that had also booked into the dinner and show. Some of the people from my tour were there, although not from my little family group, which was sad – I was by myself again.

We went to an Italian restaurant not far from the West End and enjoyed a glass of red and pasta. Our group chatted easily and comfortably, remembering all the places we had been and discussed what our favourite part of the tour was. The pain was still there, and depending on how I moved, it would hit me with a sharp stabbing pain.

After dinner, our bus and tour guide dropped us at the front of the theatre and showed us where to meet afterwards. There were people everywhere, bright lights flashing advertising the different live shows.

We found our seats and sat behind a group of Irish ladies that were in London for the weekend. They were chatty and I enjoyed listening to their accent as they did with mine. One of the girls was explaining how she was visiting Australia soon and that she was staying with relatives in Gippsland, Victoria. I knew exactly where she was going.

I was really pleased to know that we could order armchair service, including alcohol, to be delivered at the beginning of the performance or during intermission. As I was still feeling unwell, I declined the wine and decided to have an ice cream instead.

The musical show started, the singers were fantastic with amazing voices, especially the lead female singer. When Amber Riley sang *And I'm Telling You I'm Not Going*, chills ran down my back and tears were flowing down my face. Her performance was extremely moving and emotional. The night was amazing and very emotional which topped off a remarkable day.

I had changed, my life was different and I had direction.

I was up early and had breakfast with the crowd the next morning in the hotel restaurant. It was packed, extremely busy with queues everywhere to get food. As I was still in pain, I ate lightly. I checked out of the hotel and the porter hailed a cab to take me to Kensington and my new hotel for two nights. I was again by myself and really enjoyed not having to be on a schedule, or on a noisy coach, although I did miss the company of my fellow tour buddies.

As I was still in pain, I had a quiet day chillaxing after being on the go nonstop for twenty days with the tour. Furthermore, I was in excruciating pain with whatever was going on in my stomach. In hindsight, I think I should have gone to the local hospital. After arriving home and visiting my physiotherapist, he told me that a muscle had wrapped around my pancreas, nearly cutting it off.

To get on top of the pain, I wandered across the road to the local shops and found a chemist. I explained that I had this horrific pain in my side but didn't know what it was. He asked if I was all right to take codeine. I looked surprised and said 'yes'. I thought that they wouldn't sell codeine over the counter anymore as was the case in Australia. Although the pain killers were subduing the pain somewhat, my side was still hurting and I couldn't lay down properly at night to sleep.

I ended up sleeping somewhat upright with pillows piled up behind me. Unfortunately, the bed was really uncomfortable, and I had a shocking sleep with my back constantly in pain, this was on top of the pain in my side. In the morning, I went down to the hotel reception and complained that there was something wrong with the mattress. They promised to send someone up and turn it over. It certainly felt better to sleep on after that.

I had two full days in London before heading home via Singapore. I wanted to make the most of it, but the pain in my side wasn't helping matters, so I had to adjust my plans. I jumped on the tour bus for some city sightseeing, hoping to hop off and on at the sites I really wanted to see. There were two stops I really wanted to get off and explore more,

10. Ireland

the first was Kensington Gardens. Unfortunately, I really didn't have the energy to get off when the time came. The other was Harrods, and as we drove past the big brown building with the distinctive green awnings with 'Harrods' printed on them, I was a little disappointed that I was far too ill to get off the bus and walk through the famous store.

As I sat on the big bus around London, I really wanted to get off and explore – plus, I needed to go to the toilet. I jumped off at the Buckingham Palace stop and went inside the gift shop looking for a toilet. The cashier pointed me in the right direction and I made a beeline to the restroom. I then waited for another bus to drive by, so I could hop on and head back to the hotel.

As the breakfast was somewhat expensive in the hotel, I decided to wander down the street for dinner and just happened to come across a KFC takeaway. At least that helped with the hunger, although not that great for the weight. I had jumped on the scales when I first arrived in London and had dropped 8 kg after America and Paris, so I wasn't quite sure how much I had gained during the Great Britain and Ireland tour, although I didn't think it was too much as my clothes were still a bit loose on me.

I had to seriously repack my suitcase as it was full. I had trouble finding room to fit Cardboard Paul. I was definitely going home with more kilos than I arrived with.

Next time someone is going overseas and say please pack me in your suitcase, just remember that I packed Paul – although he was cardboard!

It was time to bid farewell to London but I knew I would be back. I felt at home in London, safe and knowing that I had been here in a previous life. I loved London and promised myself I would return.

11
Singapore

Day 1 – Arrival in Singapore

The London to Singapore flight was long haul with a transit in Frankfurt. The few hours stopover in Frankfurt was late at night and nothing much was open. I just sat at the gate with the rest of my fellow passengers, extremely exhausted, waiting for our flight to Singapore.

On my flight from Frankfurt to Singapore, I sat at the back of plane beside a French couple who didn't speak English, other than the wife having a minimal understanding. I was on the aisle, still in pain and tried to chat and let them know that they can just ask if they needed to get out from their seats. I was able to get some sleep until my snoring woke me up.

After waking up and realising where I was, I touched my ear and discovered that one of my new Celtic earrings bought from Waterford was missing, I was devastated but I knew they wouldn't be too far away.

Once we landed, I waited for everyone at the back of the plane to leave and then I bent down on my knees to search. My missing earring just happened to be on the floor under my seat. The relief was amazing and I was happy. After all the things that I had lost on this amazing trip, I didn't want to lose anything else. I practically skipped off the plane in happiness.

When I grabbed my luggage, it was early morning and very humid, a big difference from London.

I was greeted by a man holding a sign with my name on it. As we walked through the airport car park, there was a strong smell of incense. I spoke to the driver and he said that my experience going through customs was quick since I had no issues at all. He said that as the luggage came off the plane and into the terminal, it was scanned with security cameras. If any questionable or dubious items were found, the passenger would be pulled aside. I thought to myself, *what were they thinking when my suitcase went through with Cardboard Paul folded neatly in his calico bag?*

I was dropped off at my hotel and greeted warmly by the reception staff. I was given my key and the porter carried my bags to my room. I had a lovely view of the city and the river that meandered through the buildings. As it was morning and I only had a few days in Singapore, I wanted to get the best out of this city.

I had a hop on and off tour bus pass organised, so I went to the bus stop in front of the hotel. On my way out, the biggest thunderstorm struck with heavy rain. As it was humid and I was hot and sticky, I chanced it and ran through the rain and large puddles to get to the bus stop. I was soaked and hot, but it didn't take long to dry off. My bus arrived and I hopped on and gave the driver the letter and ticket for my pass. He told me that I had to collect the proper pass at the large shopping centre that he was heading to. I sat down and took in the sights of Singapore. On my way along the route, I made note of where I wanted to visit.

Driving through the streets, I found very different styled buildings across the city, and depending on which part of the city you were in, the architecture changed from colonial to modern. The energy also felt calm and peaceful.

We arrived at Suntec City shopping mall where I needed to collect my passes. Suntec City was the second largest shopping mall in Singapore, after VivoCity, and had over 360 retail outlets over four floors featuring brand names, department stores and plenty of restaurants. This shopping centre was massive and I decided to have a wander around at all the different shops. I was also feeling hungry and stopped off at an old familiar coffee bar, Starbucks, for the usual coffee and pastry. At least with Starbucks, the coffee all tend to taste the same, no matter which city in the world you are in. I found a food court on the ground floor and large supermarket where I could buy snacks for the hotel later.

11. Singapore

With my ticket in hand, I queued up for the bus to take me back to the hotel. Whilst waiting, I started chatting with a mother and daughter from South Coast, Sydney. I was telling them about my story, Paul's journey and travelling with Cardboard Paul. They both had tears in their eyes and I apologised for making them cry. The mother said no one would ever do that for her and commented on how amazing I was for keeping Paul's memory alive.

I arrived back at the hotel and relaxed by sitting beside the pool and keeping cool due to the heat and humidity. I also booked a massage for later that afternoon as I definitely needed one after sleeping in over forty different beds.

The massage was good and felt relaxed but I did feel like I was being pummelled to a pulp, so I was not sure if it did any good as sometimes these rough massages can put your back out. At one stage I think the masseuse walked on my back, which is not necessarily a good thing.

For dinner I decided to eat at the hotel restaurant, which was expensive with the beer costing SGD$15. I had the beef cooked in black bean sauce which was delicious.

The view at night from my hotel room was gorgeous, overlooking all the tall buildings with their lights. I slept peacefully knowing that I had one last day in this beautiful city.

Day 2 – Singapore Botanic Gardens

*I*t was my last day and I could not cram everything into the day, so I decided to walk through the beautiful Singapore Botanic Gardens.

I was getting dressed and putting on my shoes, and as I stood up, I rolled my ankle. I wasn't quite sure what was happening to me at this last stage of my trip as the pain in my side had finally subsided, but now, I had a sore ankle.

I hobbled down to the hotel reception with Cardboard Paul in his bag over my shoulder and took a photo at the front of the hotel of us in front of the lion statue. Then I hopped on the bus and headed towards the gardens.

The Singapore Botanic Gardens was created from an idea in 1822 when Sir Stamford Raffles, the founder of modern Singapore and a keen naturalist, developed the first 'Botanical and Experimental Garden' at Fort Canning. In 1859 the gardens, at its present site, was founded and created with different sections, from the National Orchid Garden to the Healing Garden and the spectacular lake with the massive lily pads.

I walked through the magnificent gardens and wandered down to the Healing Garden where different plants and herbs were grown for all different ailments and health benefits. I also walked through the rainforest section. It was hot and humid with the sweat pouring off me, my pants were soaked and stuck to my legs.

I continued to walk through these gardens and felt at peace, I could feel the energy coming from the plants and trees, enveloping me with love and peace. It was so peaceful, and I felt happy and content.

I came across a gazebo overlooking the Symphony Lake and found another photo opportunity for Cardboard Paul and me, with the lake and huge lily pads in the background. There was a waterfall near the main entrance and as Paul loved water, especially Lake Eildon and waterfalls, I thought it was fitting that I took photos of us in front of the waterfall.

When I was setting up the shot for the photo in front of the waterfall, a couple was standing not far from me and I could see the young man laughing and pointing my way. I just looked at him and smiled while his friend hit him on the arm, indicating not to be rude.

I know Paul was walking beside me throughout the gardens that day, especially when I was near the pond and the waterfall.

After taking my photos, I headed towards the gardens' café for lunch. The café faced a courtyard with water fountains in the centre spraying up water from large columns. It was hot and humid and a large thunderstorm had hovered over again with a large downpour. I was fortunate to be undercover whilst it rained heavily. After the rain, the children and ducks in the area saw it as an opportunity to play in the water. A family of ducks wandered through looking for food and being chased by the kids.

I jumped back on the bus and headed back into Suntec City to buy some Guinness for later on in the evening. I was able to sit back on the bus and take in all that Singapore had to offer. I was saddened that I didn't have enough time to really explore this beautiful city.

My ankle was still sore and swollen but I was able to walk. I had a meal of spring rolls in the restaurant for dinner before heading back to my room to pack. I also enjoyed my cold Guinness before heading to bed for an early night.

I decided to post a video on Facebook and sat down to reflect on my *#tripofalifetime* and all the experiences and memories I gathered, especially with meeting my new friends.

Day 3 – Leaving Singapore

I was up reasonably early and checked my itinerary to confirm where I had to go and at what time. I checked out of the hotel and booked a taxi to take me to Changi Airport. I advised the driver that I was flying Lufthansa Airlines and we headed for the terminal.

When I arrived, I found it difficult to find the check-in counter for the airlines as well as my flight details on the big departure information board. I finally found something that resembled the airline and went over to ask about my flight. The attendant behind the counter advised me that Lufthansa only flew late at night and that my flight was not available.

I had a slight panic and wondered what was happening, was I booked correctly? The attendant suggested I look at my itinerary again, and after looking closely I was, in fact, booked on a Singapore Airlines flight. The only problem was the gate to board my flight was in another terminal on the other side of the airport. I was fortunate that I was able to check in my luggage with the attendant and there was a train that I could take to the correct terminal.

Luckily, I had a few hours up my sleeve and enough time to get to my gate and have some lunch. I was expecting to go through customs but was surprised as this was only done at the boarding gates where bags were scanned and passports and airline tickets were checked.

Whilst walking through Changi Airport, which is massive, I noticed the unusual fashion accessories of other travellers – the blanket worn over shoulders like a jacket and neck pillows worn around the neck. It looked funny and I had a chuckle to myself.

I arrived at my gate and it was busy with other passengers queuing – the gate hadn't even opened yet. I made sure I had gone to the toilet prior to entering through security, as there were no toilets in the boarding area. I finally walked through security with no issues and sat down with all the other passengers waiting to board.

Whilst waiting, I overheard a married Australian couple discussing what they needed to do before boarding. The way they spoke to each other, particularly the women, was condescending with comments such as 'like what now', this made me feel sad. I felt like walking up to them both and saying, 'Do you really know what you have? If you lost one or the other, would you really talk to each other the way you do now?' I thought to myself, *if you were in my position, would you treat each other like this?* Losing a loved one like I did certainly gives you a different prospective and appreciation for relationships and how to respect and treat each other.

I was finally seated at the back of the plane again, and as the plane sped up, taking off and bringing me home, I became emotional, tears falling down my cheeks. I was not sure if I was sad that my *#tripofalifetime* was ending or that I was happy I was going home.

11. Singapore

All I know was that I had an incredible, life-changing experience and was bringing back a well-travelled, very tattered and creased Cardboard Paul.

12
Homeward Bound and Beyond

There is nothing like looking out the plane window as you descend and seeing your own city. I was home and happy to see Matthew and Sarah. Ollie was extremely happy to see me as well.

It was mid-morning by the time I arrived home and I threw my suitcase on my bed and started to unpack. I handed over all the souvenirs I had picked up for the kids and Ollie. I was trying to keep busy and active, not dropping off to sleep, as I wanted to acclimatise back to the local time. Although I was tired, I kept going, unpacking and putting loads of washing in the machine. It had been two weeks since I had washed any clothes, so I did have a load or two to put on.

I pulled Cardboard Paul out of the suitcase and his calico bag just to give him a breather and a stretch.

I felt totally relaxed and at peace, I was extremely calm and had never felt like this before. Sarah made a comment that I seemed different, chilled and relaxed. I wasn't sure how long it would last, but I wanted to saviour every minute of this feeling whilst it lasted.

A few days later, we celebrated what would have been Paul's 63rd birthday at a local pub with the family, including the older boys and our grandson Jordan. It was great to catch up with everyone again and show photos and chat about my tours.

After a few weeks at home, I had a clarity that I hadn't had before. Ideas for my new business was flowing easily with incredible details of what my new life and business looked like.

I was also feeling sad and flat as I was home and wasn't travelling anywhere. Pauline and I kept in touch and started planning our next trip for May 2018. I had a feeling to head up to Uluru in central Australia and contacted Alyssa again to organise a week for Pauline and me. Unfortunately, the cost to travel within Australia was far more expensive than to travel overseas, so Pauline and I decided that it was time to look somewhere else. We eventually chose to travel to Phuket for ten days and even took Cardboard Paul with us.

In early 2018, I brought together a group of like-minded women to join me in supporting each other in our businesses and run workshops with a monthly theme based on mind, body and spirit. The concept was great, but unfortunately after six months, it didn't really take off. I ended up cancelling all the planned workshops. It was disappointing but I knew that I was being guided in another direction. Although I wasn't quite sure what it was, I knew that Cardboard Paul may have something to do with it.

Since taking Cardboard Paul around the world, he has made several appearances at the *Being Connected* workshops, the open mic nights at Busybird Publishing and my new workplace. Each time I introduce Cardboard Paul, he is greeted warmly, and our story often brings a laugh or big smile on people's faces – as well as the occasional tear.

I have kept in touch with some of my USA tour family, catching up with my Melbourne friend, Lynda, for the odd dinner and live show. In November 2018, Lynda and I visited Margo in Wangaratta for the blues festival over a weekend.

And of course, my sister Pauline from Perth, who I have travelled to Phuket with in May 2018 and now booked to travel together to Edinburgh in August 2019, where we are planning to take an upgraded Cardboard Paul on tour with us.

I have kept in contact with my tour family from the Great Britain and Ireland tour over Facebook and e-mail as well:

Lisa: *At first it seemed unusual seeing Cardboard Paul but then I remember thinking what a great way to have him with you for some closure. I would never have thought to do that. It was a promise kept to travel together. Yours was so raw and recent, and over 12 years had passed for me, but I saw the comfort it brought you. After a while he was just part of the tour. I, too, have some fun pics of you two, especially the one near Buckingham Palace when I first saw him. That caused a second look, ha!*

Lisa also sent an e-mail out to the group thanking everyone for making her time on the tour enjoyable. She thanked me for introducing Paul.

12. Homeward Bound and Beyond

Considering she lost her husband over 12 years ago, she knows the struggles of losing a husband. Lisa has been showing everyone the photos of the two of us and they think Paul and I are a hoot.

Becky: *I hope you and Paul will inspire others as well to take those trips, because we really don't know what life will bring us.*

Gail: *Since I am so brilliant and ever so clever, I would be delighted for you to share my extraordinary humour in your book! Be sure to mention me as your inspiration! Hans, the stable one in our relationship, also says yes! I look forward to reading both of your books!*

Janet and Wayne: *Wayne made a slideshow of our UK trip and we had it playing at our Christmas party and have shown it several times as well. We always point out Cardboard Paul. He causes quite a stir, especially amongst our Uruguayan friends who have never heard of such a thing. One of them asked for the picture at Anne Hathaway's cottage so she could send it to all her friends and tell them about him.*

I was extremely fortunate to be able to travel on this *#tripofalifetime* while keeping a promise to Paul. In doing so, this journey has been life-changing and I have connected with some beautiful people that I now call friends. I am forever blessed and look forward to travelling again, especially with Cardboard Paul, continuing to keep his memory alive and creating new memories for me and others that I encounter.

Life is too short, you have got to grab it, run with it, move forward and live to its fullest.

I am forever grateful for Paul's death because from his death came opportunities and wonderful experiences that I may not have had if Paul were still with me. I wouldn't have written *Conversations with Paul* or travelled overseas with his cardboard cut-out, which provided another opportunity to write about our adventures. I wouldn't have met the wonderful people over the past three years. So, I am forever grateful as we never know what our today, tomorrow or future holds.

I am also grateful that I kept my promise to him.

About the Author

Michelle Bourke is a storyteller who writes about true life – from losing her beloved husband, Paul, to cancer to recreating her life without him by her side. Michelle was born and raised in Melbourne and married her soul mate in 1991. They raised their two children in their home in Taylors Lakes.

After Paul's death in May 2016, Michelle wrote *Conversations with Paul*, a story about a journey of love, heartache, frustration and determination whilst facing a loved one's terminal illness.

Michelle has travelled around the world with a cardboard cut-out of Paul, keeping promises and writing stories of her amazing experiences.

Her ability to be real and authentic whilst honouring Paul's memory and keeping true to herself has inspired the many people she has met. Michelle has been called courageous but remains humble in all that she does.

To connect with or learn more about Michelle, visit:

www.beingconnected.com.au

www.conversationswithpaul.com.au

www.michellebourke.com.au

USA Tour

London Tour

Scotland – Ireland

Singapore

www.ingramcontent.com/pod-product-compliance
Lightning Source LLC
Chambersburg PA
CBHW021102080526
44587CB00010B/343